# A FIELD GUIDE TO
# TEXAS SNAKES

Trans Pecos Rat Snake
*Elaphe subocularis*

# A FIELD GUIDE TO
# TEXAS SNAKES

## by Alan Tennant

Contributing Authors
John E. Werler and Bill Marvel

Photography
Michael J. Bowerman

Maps
Craig McIntyre

Identification Key
A. J. Seippel

**Gulf Publishing Company**
Houston, Texas

Gulf Publishing Company
Book Division
P.O. Box 2608 ☐ Houston, Texas 77252-2608

10 9 8 7 6 5

*Texas Monthly* is a registered trademark of Mediatex Communications Corporation.

**Library of Congress Cataloging-in-Publication Data**

Tennant, Alan, 1943–
  A field guide to Texas snakes/by Alan Tennant; contributing authors, John E. Werler and Bill Marvel; photography, Michael J. Bowerman; maps, Craig McIntyre; identification key, A. J. Seippel.
     p.    cm.
  Includes index.
  ISBN 0-932012-97-3(hbk).—ISBN 0-87719-012-7 (pbk)
  1. Snakes—Texas—Identification. I. Werler, John E. II. Marvel, Bill.
III. Title.
QL666.06T457    1990
597.96'09764—dc20                                             90-13226
                                                              CIP

Technical illustrations by John Lockman

Book design by Larry Smitherman

Printed in Hong Kong

# CONTENTS

5

# *PREFACE*

Johns Hopkins paleontologist Robert T. Bakker once observed that only with considerable difficulty had he been able to gain a perspective from which a thecodont—a stubby little Jurassic reptile shaped like a fireplug—seemed as beautiful as a cheetah. The thecodont just had a different environment, to which it adapted by squatting on the shores of ancient mud pans, gobbling down frogs and other amphibians, and living in the same workable give-and-take with its neighbors that, infinitely extrapolated across the panoply of living beings, reveals a system of balances so intricately poised and delicately counterweighted that only a bit of its circuitry is yet available to our understanding. The system's essence, however, is clear: cosmologically complex sets of opposing hungers and wills-to-live suspend each life form in a tenuous equilibrium somewhere between dominance over its environment and extinction.

In this unconscious genetic struggle, each species' individual capacities and élan contribute to the natural forces massed against its prey, its predators, and many of its neighbors, whose efforts, collectively asserted, oppose the creature's own drive for biological success just enough to allow all of them to exist, balanced, in communities ranging from that of a drop of water to those carpeting the Great Plains. Most of the time, this system of opposing interests maintains a fluctuating but enduring stasis, steadily replacing dropout species with sudden efflorescences from neighboring life forms, which immediately venture evolutionary tendrils into every vacated environmental space.

As little more than blinking spectators to the process, the least we can do is respect the contenders, although nothing could be further from our historical record, especially where snakes are concerned. We generally don't eat them, some of them can kill us, and in the prevailing cultural context most are so scary that even to people who would hesitate to harm any other vertebrate, it has long seemed proper to kill a serpent. Yet, with the passing of so many animals that threatened first our lives, then our livestock, that viewpoint is slowly changing. Only recently have we come to see how much we've lost in ridding ourselves of the bears and wolves, mountain lions and alligators and snakes we so recently saw merely as villains. Too late, for the most part, an awareness has dawned not only of the biological magnitude of their loss but of the fundamental arrogance in judging fellow competitors by the norms of our provincial human notions of good and evil, beauty and ugliness—as though such standards could be relevant to a system of harmonies that preceded our existence by billions of years and will certainly outlast us by an equivalent span. To choose certain striking beings— cheetahs, swallows, or redwood trees—to grace with our newly acquired aesthetic values is to ignore how meagerly this concept stacks up against a cosmic order whose structure binds the stately parade of stars and planets, shapes the tectonic currents that mold the continents, and has wrought the symmetry of serpents no less than of tigers.

Casting reptiles into roles created mainly by our need to assign malfeasance to beings we perceive as psychologically alien, moreover, traps us within the illusion that our species is a separate, higher entity, and hides from us our essence as no more than another thread in the same organic tapesty—a matrix in which every single species of us is inextricably bound to the others by myriad, dovetailing pacts not of our own making but on which, nevertheless, our joint survival ultimately depends.

# ACKNOWLEDGMENTS

$M$y sincere thanks to: mapmaker, editor, and consultant Craig McIntyre.

Those who graciously and laboriously read, corrected, and commented at length on the manuscript for this book: Dave Barker, Dallas Zoo; Neil B. Ford, University of Texas at Tyler; Chris Kindschi; William W. Lamar, University of Texas at Tyler; Jim Stout, Caldwell Zoo; and A. J. Seippel.

Those whose generosity with their time and knowledge made *The Snakes of Texas* possible: Joseph M. Abell, M.D., Michael Allender, Jim Ashcraft, Paul Bartlett, Bob Binder, Johnny Binder, W. F. Blair, Bryan Blake, Dave Blody, Jim Bull, Patrick Burchfield, Susan Burneson, Chris Carson, Holly Carver, Cathy Casey, Bill Dagenhart, Carolyn Davis, Barbara Dillingham, Anne Dirkes, Jim Dunlap, David Easterla, Rowe Elliott, Richard Etheridge, Jan Faulk, Joe Forks, Jim George, Thomas Glass, M.D., Jerry Glidewell, Charles Goodrich, Tony Granes, Ed Guidry, David M. Hardy, M.D., Richard Hix, Erik Holmback, Dan Howell, Richard Hudson, Burrell Johnston, J. P. Jones, John Jones, Tim Jones, Tommy Jones, Jack Joy, Alan Kardon, Bill King, Robert E. Kuntz, Bob Lange, Jozsef Laszlo, David L. Lindsey, W. E. Lockhart, M.D., Scott Lubeck, Connie McIntyre, Jeff McIntyre, Ray Meckel, Susie and S. I. Morris, the late Eileen Morron, Cindy Nations, Nick Nevid, Dan Okrent, Floyd Potter, Rick Pratt, Hugh Quinn, Gus Rentfro, Francis Rose, Findlay E. Russell, M.D., Barbara Scown, Dean Singleton, Ken Smith, Larry and Marlene Smitherman, Linda Stout, Jeannie Taylor, Joe Teska, Luke Thompson, Dennis Trost, M.D., Earl Turner, Thomas Vermersch, Rocky Ward, Brett Whitney, Michael A. Williamson, Sherri Williamson, Larry David Wilson, Margaret Wilson, Richard Wilson, Tom Wood, Richard Worthington, and Jim Yantis.

Artists John Lockman and David Moellendorf.

Photographers Michael Allender, Dave Barker, Ted L. Brown, Donna Marvel, D. Craig McIntyre, George O. Miller, and Robert Wayne Van Devender.

I would like to acknowledge my debt to Roger Conant's *A Field Guide to the Reptiles and Amphibians of Eastern and Central North America* (Boston: Houghton Mifflin, 1975) as the source of many of the record lengths cited in this volume; further, the fine line drawings of the late Isabelle Hunt Conant served as source material for a number of John Lockman's black-and-white illustrations.

# FOREWORD

Benjamin Tharp's *The Vegetation of Texas* (1939), Frank Blair's *The Biotic Provinces of Texas* (1950), and a synthesis of modern distributional data suggest that Texas has six natural regions and ten community types (italicized):

1. The eastern Forest Region, principally composed of a *pine-hardwood forest* fringed on the west by the *oak-hickory forest* called the Cross Timbers in North Central Texas.

2. The central and coastal Prairie Region, denoted by *tallgrass prairie*, which is known as blackland prairie in Central Texas.

3. The Tamaulipan Region of South Texas, comprising both tall-grass and *shortgrass prairie* interspersed with clumps of woody plants that form *thorn woodland*, locally named chaparral or simply brush.

4. The Edwards Plateau Region of Central Texas, containing both shortgrass prairie and oak-juniper *evergreen woodland*, locally called cedar brakes.

5. The High Plains Region of West Texas, especially the Pan-handle, covered with shortgrass prairie but broken by mesas and canyons with evergreen woodland.

6. The Chihuahuan Desert Region of Trans-Pecos Texas, which includes *shrub desert* in low basins, shortgrass prairie on the rolling plains above, *succulent desert* and evergreen woodland on the lower and upper mountain slopes, respectively, and *coniferous forest* on a few high peaks.

*Riparian or deciduous woodland* follows creeks and rivers through all natural community types of the state.

Thirty-six percent of the 68 snake species in Texas are of eastern derivation. They range widely in eastern or southeastern North America but reach western limits in Texas, where most are stopped by either the arid western plateaus or the shortgrass prairie of the High Plains. The eastern hognose snake, the Texas rat snake, and the timber rattlesnake are examples.

The second important group of snakes (23 percent of the state's species) is basically western or southwestern, with eastern limits in Texas set by the central tallgrass prairie; the ground snake, the long-nose snake, and the prairie rattlesnake are among this group.

Additionally, there exists a small number (14 percent) of central North American or Great Plains species such as the Texas blind snake, the central and Texas lined snakes, and the western hognose snake; a yet smaller group (9 percent) is of Chihuahuan regional derivation, among which are the Trans-Pecos rat snake, the western hooknose snake, and the rock rattlesnake. A few (9 percent) trans-continental species also range across Texas, including ringneck snakes, desert and speckled kingsnakes, and several garter snakes, while some essentially tropical snakes, such as the indigo, cat-eyed, and black-striped snakes, reach the northern limits of their range in the state's Tamaulipan Region. A single endemic, the Harter's water snake, is found entirely within Texas.

James Rogers (1976) recently analyzed these distributions and found that vertical landscape diversity and the number of coexisting small-mammal species were the chief positive influences on the number of local snake species. High altitude has a significant nega-tive effect, however. The diverse ophidian population of the eastern and central portions of the state is, of course, the result of the strong eastern faunal element, but Texas' overall diversity is due to the ad-dition of numerous western serpents plus the mix of important spe-cialties from the Great Plains, Chihuahuan Desert, and Tamaulipan regions, and no other state has as many snake species.

Frederick R. Gehlbach
*Baylor University*

# A FIELD GUIDE TO
# TEXAS SNAKES

# VENOM POISONING

W. C. Fields liked to tell people he always kept some whiskey handy in case he saw a snake—which he also kept handy. Few people still employ Fields' favorite remedy, but most are unaware that following the standard, generally sanctioned first aid procedures for snakebite is usually more dangerous than doing nothing at all. Without question, one shouldn't cut open a bite wound to suck out the venom: even under the best of circumstances this classical regimen is of more harm than value. Moreover, except in the most remote wilderness areas there is ordinarily plenty of time to get to a hospital, for unlike chemical poisoning, even the most serious envenomations by North American snakes seldom assume life-threatening severity for at least several hours.[1] Therefore it's better to concentrate on getting good medical management than to fumble with dangerous field incisions; merely to immobilize an envenomated extremity, remove rings or shoes before swelling takes place, wrap the limb firmly in a splinted elastic bandage, and then get the victim to a good hospital is to do nothing wrong and the most important part of what's right.[2]

Most of the wrong comes from binding the limb with thin, circulation-cutting cord or cutting open the punctures, both of which destroy nerve and muscle tissue by aiming to drain the venom away or to prevent its transit throughout the body by severely restricting the flow of blood through the area. Neither of these is a workable strategy because they are founded on a basic misunderstanding of

17

the complex biological process that begins when a venomous snake bites a human being: that a strike by one of these animals results in the injection of a dollop of lethal fluid that then oozes slowly through the vascular system toward the heart.[3]

Because of their large molecular structure, though, most of the numerous components of pit viper venom are dispersed primarily through the lymph system rather than by the flow of blood, making for a comparatively slow, general diffusion best impeded by firmly wrapping the bitten area in an elastic bandage, splinting it in place, then rewrapping the entire limb to immobilize it. This allows cellular oxygen exchange, while the broad pressure of the elastic bandage compresses the lymph vessels enough to inhibit the muscular-contraction-pumped spread of the venom-saturated lymphatic fluid. Referred to as the Australian method because it was developed as a field treatment for the bites of that continent's large population of deadly serpents, this therapy has also proven effective in the first aid treatment of envenomation by North American pit vipers. And it dovetails perfectly with the medical consensus concerning subsequent hospital management of reptile envenomation—a campaign that relies heavily on the intravenous administration of antivenin combined with antihistamines to stifle allergic reaction. Proponents of this approach maintain that not only are the life-threatening systemic failures that may follow major poisoning best offset by antivenin antibodies, but the serum offers the only significant means of mitigating the often extensive local death of tissue caused by pit viper toxins.

The reason such necrosis is high near the wound is that killing prey is only the preliminary function of snake venom; most of its 12 to 30 peptides and enzymes are devoted to digestion. Within the bodies of human beings bitten by rattlesnakes, cottonmouths, and copperheads, therefore, just as in the snakes' rodent prey, these enzymes simply disintegrate the living tissues. (Like all digestive processes, it is both complicated and quick—the viper's normal prey is so fleet that a snake whose venom doesn't drop its meal within yards stands a good chance of losing it altogether.) Moreover, because the toxic proteins of snake venom are structurally similar to those of the victim's own cells, within seconds of injection they incorporate themselves into his blood and tissues, for all practical purposes simply becoming part of the body. Any attempt to extract these reptilian enzymes in the field is therefore useless, and even in the hospital surgical removal of the entire bite area does little to offset the venom's ultimate lethal effect.

Nor is surgically opening a limb in fasciotomy often necessary, as was formerly believed, to offset the pressure of edema, or swelling. Despite the often distorted proportions of an envenomated limb, swelling seldom threatens the life of the limb because the distension is usually soft and limited to the epidermal and outer cutaneous layers. Here, even severe edema almost never cuts off circulation like a hydraulic tourniquet, and only rarely does enough deep pressure occur to impair blood flow and oxygen exchange. Yet among less sophisticated Texas doctors fasciotomy is commonly initiated on both this misconception and the notion that leaving a limb opened for several days facilitates drainage of its venom-saturated tissues. Reptile toxins simply do not flow out of tissue to which they have metabolically bonded, however, and leaving a limb surgically breached for this length of time risks infection, nerve damage, and the loss of postrecovery flexion due to scarring. In treating some 200 venomous snakebites, Ken Mattox and his team at Houston's Ben Taub Hospital have used fasciotomy to relieve hydraulic tourniqueting less than a half-dozen times, while Findlay Russell of the University of Arizona, who has seen more cases of reptilian envenomation than anyone else in North America, has never had to perform a fasciotomy due to excessive intracompartmental pressure.

Some authorities on envenomation by both native and exotic reptiles are:

Joseph M. Abell, M.D., Austin

David Feliciano, M.D., Ben Taub Hospital, Houston

Thomas C. Glass, Jr., M.D., Clinical Associate Professor of Surgery, University of Texas Medical School, San Antonio

David L. Hardy, M.D., Arizona Poison Control System, or Coagulation Research Laboratory, Department of Pediatrics, University of Arizona Health Sciences Center, Tucson, Arizona

Ronald Jones, M.D., Parkland Hospital, Dallas

George Jordan, M.D., Ben Taub Hospital, Houston

W. E. Lockhart, M.D., Alpine

Ken Mattox, M.D., Ben Taub Hospital, Houston

Sherman A. Minton, M.D., Department of Biology, Indiana University Medical Center, Bloomington, Indiana

Findlay E. Russell, M.D., Ph.D., Department of Pharmacology and Toxicology, University of Arizona, Tucson

L.H.S. Van Mierop, M.D., Department of Pediatrics (Cardiology), University of Florida Medical School, Gainesville, Florida

Charles H. Watt, Jr., M.D., Archbold Memorial Hospital, Thomasville, Georgia

---

1. An exception is the sudden, intense allergic reaction a few people experience in response to even minimal infusion of any animal toxin, such as those present in bee or wasp stings; another is the rare case of vascular collapse brought on by the chance injection of a large amount of snake venom directly into a major vein. Children, because of their much smaller volume of body fluid available to absorb the toxins and to accommodate the plasma leakage brought about by its enzymes' perforation of their capillaries, are more vulnerable to venom poisoning than adults, although there is still usually sufficient time to reach a hospital. (The same is true even for small dogs, which tend to be resistant to pit viper poisoning; cats are less tolerant of its effects.)

2. An ice pack on the bound wound and another on the victim's forehead may ease the pain a bit and help to mitigate the waves of nausea that often accompany envenomation by rattlesnakes, the cottonmouth, and the copperhead.

3. Severe envenomation doesn't always accompany a bite, however, and even punctures by the hot-tempered pit vipers are largely free of toxins about a fifth of the time, while fewer than half of coral snake bites result in serious poisoning. Nevertheless, where a coral has clearly broken the skin, a temporary (of less than thirty minutes' duration) arterial tourniquet is probably advisable, since this animal's peptide-based venom spreads far more rapidly than the toxins of pit vipers.

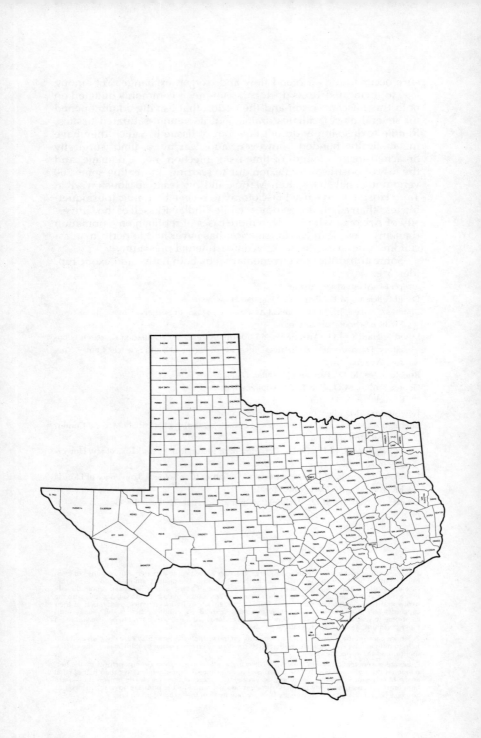

# INTRODUCTION

The common and scientific names used here follow the nomenclature established by the Society for the Study of Amphibians and Reptiles in J. T. Collins, et al., *Standard Common and Current Scientific Names for North American Amphibians and Reptiles* (Lawrence, Kan.: Society for the Study of Amphibians and Reptiles, 1982).

The order in which the snakes appear in the book reflects primarily their resemblance to other similarly sized and patterned serpents, or their occupancy of similar habitat niches—aquatic snakes, for example. Every species and subspecies that occurs in Texas is described, but several of those whose differences from more common races are either entirely internal (the Mexican blackhead snake) or so slight as to be imperceptible in a photograph are not pictured. (The number assigned to each animal in the text is also used in the photograph captions and the index.)

The range maps accompanying the text are an attempt to define the distribution of these animals. The dark-shaded portion of each map represents the general distribution of a particular subspecies; since the precise geographical range of most subspecies has not been formally determined, however, these demarcations are merely approximations. The more lightly shaded regions on some of the maps indicate intergradation—areas where the ranges of two or more subspecies overlap. Genetic crosses found in these areas often exhibit characteristics of each of the subspecies involved. (Since many of the exact zones of intergradation between adjacently ranging subspecies are also yet to be conclusively established, specimens occurring near the line dividing the two subspecies' ranges may likewise show intergrade characteristics of both forms.)

Even within their geographic ranges, snakes are likely to occur only where proper environmental conditions and habitat exist; a subspecies may be quite common in some parts of its range, yet very rare or absent in other places well within its overall geographical distribution. The map on page 20 has been included to assist in locating particular counties mentioned in the text as areas where a subspecies is relatively abundant.

In the future, many subspecies will undoubtedly be found in areas where they are currently unrecorded; factors such as habitat alteration are also likely to cause local extirpation of numerous subspecies while allowing others to expand their ranges.

Published material used, in part, in compiling the distribution areas of the maps includes G. G. Raun and F. R. Gehlbach, *Amphibians and Reptiles in Texas* (Dallas: Dallas Museum of Natural History, 1972); Herpetological Review, vols. 3–13; K. L. Williams, *Systematics and Natural History of the American Milk Snake*, Lampropeltis triangulum (Milwaukee: Milwaukee Public Museum Press, 1978); J. Glidewell, Southwestern Naturalist 19 (2):213–23, 1974; D. Miller, "A Life History Study of the Gray-banded Kingsnake, *Lampropeltis mexicana alterna*, in Texas" (master's thesis, Sul Ross State University, 1979); J. E. Werler, *Poisonous Snakes of Texas and the First Aid Treatment of Their Bites* (Austin: Texas Parks and Wildlife, 1978); R. Conant, *A Field Guide to Reptiles and Amphibians of Eastern and Central North America* (Boston: Houghton-Mifflin, 1975) and Journal of Herpetology 11 (2):217–20, 1977; C. J. Cole and L. M. Hardy, Bulletin of the American Museum of Natural History, vol. 171, 1981; and J. S. Mecham, Copeia 1956:51–52.

Others who assisted with advice, field records, and additional distribution data are Craig, Connie, and Jeff McIntyre; Earl Turner; Neil Ford; Terry Hibbitts, Jr.; Jim Stout; Jack Joy; Michael Allender; Bill and Donna Marvel; Thomas Vermersch; and Frederick R. Gehlbach.

# SCALATION

## Head Scales: Nonvenomous Snake

internasal — supraocular

prefrontal — frontal — parietal

postoculars
supraocular — anterior temporal
preoculars — posterior temporal
prefrontal
internasal — upper labials
rostral — lower labials
nasal — loreal

mental — anterior chin shields
posterior chin shields
gulars — ventrals

## Head Scales: Pit Viper

supraocular — canthals — prenasal
preoculars — postnasal
pit
rostral
mental
upper labials — chin shields
lower labials

loreals
canthals — supraocular
postnasal — postoculars
nostril
pit
rostral
prenasal — preoculars — upper labials
lower labials

lower labials — gulars
mental
chin shields — ventrals

## Undertail:
## Nonvenomous Snake

Note: The nonvenomous Texas longnose snake
has a single row of subcaudal scales.

## Undertail:
## Pit Viper

Note: The venomous coral snake has a double
row of subcaudal scales.

numbering of dorsal
scale rows

smooth scales

keeled scales

divided anal plate

single anal plate

# IDENTIFICATION KEY

People who do a lot of looking at plants or animals develop a seemingly amazing ability to identify them from the merest glance. Typically, rather than instantly picking out the specimen's specific, subtle identifying characteristics, these people are recognizing the unique group of static and kinetic attributes that together make up what might be thought of as the creature's visual gestalt. This skill comes only after seeing a great many similar plants or animals, however, and until it is acquired, about the only way to distinguish difficult species is through the use of a taxonomic key.

This one is a tool to aid in the identification of most snakes found in the state. (It is, of course, possible to encounter the rare serpent not typical of its genus, such as an albino.) All numbered questions should be answered in sequence: a Yes answer to the first question leads to question 2. Where more than one question is asked, all answers must be Yes to take the Yes option. A magnifying glass may be helpful in picking out details of scalation, particularly when identifying small snakes.

If it is difficult to answer a question, assume the answer is Yes and continue to the end. If the snake is not the one described in the text, return to the doubtful question and take the No option, continuing through the key until the correct genus can be established. Beyond genus level, the photographs, text, and distribution maps will establish a particular animal's species and subspecies.

1. Is the body covered with small dry scales? Does the animal lack legs, fins, movable eyelids, and external ear openings?

yes ..................................................................... 2
no .............................................................. Not a snake.

2. Is there a pit (depression) on the side of the head, between the eye and the nostril?

nostril

vertical pupil (cat eye)

pit

yes ....................................................................... 3
no ...................................................................... 10

3. Does the snake have a single row of scales under the tail? Does it have vertical pupils, like a cat's eyes?

single row                                    anal plate

yes ........................................................................ 4
no .......... You have reached this point in error; return to question 2

4. Are there rattles at the end of the tail?

rattles

yes ........................................................................ 5
no ........................................................................ 9

5. Are there 8 or fewer large scales and many small granular scales on the top of the head?

yes ........................................................................ 6
no ........................................................................ 7

6. This is a rattlesnake of the genus *Crotalus* (101–107).

7. Are there 9 large scales on top of the head?

yes ........................................................................ 8
no .......... You have reached this point in error; return to question 4

8. This is a rattlesnake of the genus *Sistrurus* (108–110).

9. This is a copperhead or cottonmouth of the genus *Agkistrodon* (97–100).

10. Is the snake red, yellow, and black, with the colors arranged in bands that completely encircle the body? Are the red and black bands noticeably wider than the yellow bands, with the red and yellow bands touching?

yes ......................................................... 11
no .......................................................... 12

11. This is a Texas coral snake, genus *Micrurus* (96).

12. Does the snake resemble a worm: tiny, pinkish or flesh-colored, with a blunt tail and eyes that appear to be small, almost invisible dots? Are the scales on the belly not much wider than those on the back?

yes ......................................................... 13
no .......................................................... 14

13. This is a blind snake of the genus *Leptotyphlops* (1–3).

14. Are all the dorsal (back) scales entirely smooth (not keeled or ridged)?

smooth scales          keeled scales

yes ......................................................... 15
no .......................................................... 61

15. Is the snake quite small, and is the tip of its snout upturned? Are there 17 rows of dorsal scales at midbody?

upturned snout          numbering of dorsal scale rows

yes ......................................................... 16
no .......................................................... 19

16. Is the top of the head patterned with 1 or 2 prominent blackish bands?

yes ......................................................... 17
no .......................................................... 18

17. This is a western hooknose snake, genus *Gyalopion* (48).

18. This is a Mexican hooknose snake, genus *Ficimia* (49).

19. Turn the animal over to locate the anal plate, which covers the vent and is located about two thirds of the way to the tail tip. Is the anal plate single (undivided)?

single anal plate          divided anal plate

yes ......................................................... 20
no .......................................................... 30

20. Is the snake uniformly black above, with 17 rows of dorsal scales at midbody?

yes ......................................................... 21
no .......................................................... 22

21. This is a Texas indigo snake, genus *Drymarchon* (70).

22. Does the animal have a single row of scales under the tail and 23 rows of dorsal scales at midbody?

single row                    anal plate

yes ......................................................... 23
no .......................................................... 24

23. This is a Texas longnose snake, genus *Rhinocheilus* (88).

24. Is the belly white or yellowish without any brown or other dark markings?

yes ......................................................... 25
no .......................................................... 29

25. Are there 8 lower labial scales, and are the back and sides colored red, black, and off-white?

yes ......................................................... 26
no .......................................................... 27

26. This is a scarlet snake of the genus *Cemophora* (94–95).

27. Is the dorsal color off-white blotched with brown? Is there a pale longitudinal line along the spine just behind the head? Are there 12 to 15 lower labial scales?

yes ......................................................... 28
no .......... You have reached this point in error; return to question 2

28. This is a glossy snake of the genus *Arizona* (53–55).

29. This is a kingsnake or milk snake of the genus *Lampropeltis* (43, 56–57, 89–93).

30. Are there 17 or fewer rows of dorsal scales at midbody?

yes ......................................................... 31
no .......................................................... 50

31. Is the snake longitudinally striped, and does it have an enlarged, triangular-shaped rostral scale that curves back over the snout and has free edges?

rostral scale

yes ........................................................ 32
no ......................................................... 33

32. This is a patchnose snake of the genus *Salvadora* (34–36).

33. Is the snake small, with a slender body, a tiny head, a solid brown back, and 15 rows of dorsal scales at midbody? Does it lack a loreal scale?

loreal scale          loreal scale absent

yes ........................................................ 34
no ......................................................... 35

34. This is a blackhead, blackhood, or flathead snake of the genus *Tantilla* (7–12).

35. Are there 2 or more preocular scales?

preocular scales

yes ........................................................ 36
no ......................................................... 45

36. Are the lower and upper preocular scales about the same size?

yes ........................................................ 37
no ......................................................... 40

37. Is the nasal plate divided? Is the animal slate gray above, with a darker head and a black-speckled orangish belly?

divided nasal plate

yes ........................................................ 38
no ......................................................... 39

38. This is a ringneck snake of the genus *Diadophis* (4–6).

39. This is a western smooth green snake, genus *Opheodrys* (38).

40. Is the animal quite slender for its length, and are there 15 rows of dorsal (back) scales counted at midbody?

yes ........................................................ 41
no ......................................................... 42

41. This is a whipsnake of the genus *Masticophis* (60–63).

42. Are there 17 rows of dorsal scales at midbody, and 13 rows just ahead of the anal plate?

yes ........................................................ 43
no ......................................................... 44

43. This is a coachwhip of the genus *Masticophis* (58–59).

44. This is a racer of the genus *Coluber* (64–68).

45. Is the loreal scale in direct contact with the eye?

loreal scale

yes ......................................................... 46
no .......................................................... 49

46. Is the back black, the lower sides pinkish? Are there fewer than 15 rows of dorsal scales at midbody?
yes ......................................................... 47
no .......................................................... 48

47. This is a western worm snake, genus *Carphophis* (22).

48. This is a western smooth earth snake, genus *Virginia* (20).

49. This is a ground snake, genus *Sonora* (19).

50. Is the animal shiny black above and pink below, with a horny point on the tip of its tail?
yes ......................................................... 51
no .......................................................... 52

51. This is a western mud snake, genus *Farancia* (82).

52. Is the snake quite slender, and are its eyes proportionately very large, with vertical (cat-eyed) pupils?
yes ......................................................... 53
no .......................................................... 58

53. Are the back and sides light brown or buff narrowly banded with darker brown, and are 2 or more loreal scales present?
yes ......................................................... 54
no .......................................................... 55

54. This is a Texas lyre snake, genus *Trimorphodon* (86).

55. Are the back and sides yellowish, with wide, blackish-brown bands? Is the undertail orange or salmon?
yes ......................................................... 56
no .......................................................... 57

56. This is a northern cat-eyed snake, genus *Leptodeira* (87).

57. This is a night snake of the genus *Hypsiglena* (83–84).

58. Is the snake small and slender, its back and sides longitudinally striped with black and brown? Are there 19 rows of dorsal scales at midbody?

yes ........................................................ 59
no ......................................................... 60

59. This is a black-striped snake, genus *Coniophanes* (85).

60. This is a rat snake of the genus *Elaphe* (39–42).

61. Is the snake comparatively plump, with a snout whose tip is distinctly upturned? Are there 23 to 25 rows of dorsal (back) scales counted at midbody?

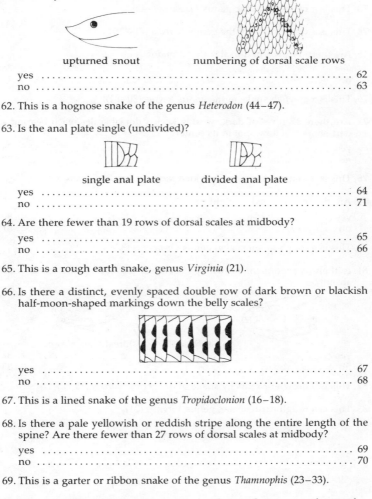

upturned snout        numbering of dorsal scale rows

yes ........................................................ 62
no ......................................................... 63

62. This is a hognose snake of the genus *Heterodon* (44–47).

63. Is the anal plate single (undivided)?

single anal plate       divided anal plate

yes ........................................................ 64
no ......................................................... 71

64. Are there fewer than 19 rows of dorsal scales at midbody?

yes ........................................................ 65
no ......................................................... 66

65. This is a rough earth snake, genus *Virginia* (21).

66. Is there a distinct, evenly spaced double row of dark brown or blackish half-moon-shaped markings down the belly scales?

yes ........................................................ 67
no ......................................................... 68

67. This is a lined snake of the genus *Tropidoclonion* (16–18).

68. Is there a pale yellowish or reddish stripe along the entire length of the spine? Are there fewer than 27 rows of dorsal scales at midbody?

yes ........................................................ 69
no ......................................................... 70

69. This is a garter or ribbon snake of the genus *Thamnophis* (23–33).

70. This is a bullsnake, Louisiana pine snake, or Sonoran gopher snake, genus *Pituophis* (50–52).

71. Are there 21 or more rows of dorsal scales at midbody?

yes ........................................................................ 72
no ......................................................................... 75

72. Are at least the scales along the spine weakly keeled, and does the flat belly meet the rather vertical (rather than laterally bulging) sides of the slender body at an abrupt angle (like a loaf of bread in cross-section)?

yes ........................................................................ 73
no ......................................................................... 74

73. This is a rat snake of the genus *Elaphe* (39–42).

74. This is a water snake of the genus *Nerodia* (71–79).

75. Are there 19 rows of dorsal scales at midbody?

yes ........................................................................ 76
no ......................................................................... 77

76. This is a crayfish snake of the genus *Regina* (80–81).

77. Are there 17 rows of dark, weakly keeled dorsal scales, each bearing a dart-shaped yellow spot in its center?

yes ........................................................................ 78
no ......................................................................... 79

78. This is a Central American speckled racer, genus *Drymobius* (69).

79. Are the back and sides bright green?

yes ........................................................................ 80
no ......................................................................... 81

80. This is a rough green snake, genus *Opheodrys* (37).

81. Is there a prominent brown spot beneath the eye? Is the loreal scale absent?

loreal scale          loreal scale absent

yes ........................................................................ 82
no ......................................................................... 83

82. This is a brown or redbelly snake of the genus *Storeria* (13–15).

83. This is a rough earth snake, genus *Virginia* (21).

*Plains blind snake*

**3**   *Trans-Pecos blind snake*

**4** *Mississippi ringneck snake*

**5** *Prairie ringneck snake*

34

**6**  *Regal ringneck snake*

*Flathead snake*

**8**  *Plains blackhead snake*

**9**  *Southwestern blackhead snake*

**11**   *Devil's River blackhead snake*

**2**   *Blackhood snake*

**13**  *Texas brown snake*

**14**  *Marsh brown snake*

**15**  *Southern redbelly snake*

**16**  *Texas lined snake*

**17** *Central lined snake*

**19** *Ground snake*

**19**  *Ground snake*

**19**  *Ground snake*

**20** *Western smooth earth snake*

**21** *Rough earth snake*

**22**  *Western worm snake*

**23**  *Eastern garter snake*

**24** *Texas garter snake*

**25** *New Mexico garter snake*

**6** *Western plains garter snake*

**27** *Checkered garter snake*

**28**   *Eastern blackneck garter snake*

**29**   *Western blackneck garter snake*

**30** *Western ribbon snake*

**31** *Redstripe ribbon snake*

**32**  *Gulf Coast ribbon snake*

**33**  *Arid land ribbon snake*

**34** *Texas patchnose snake*

**35** *Mountain patchnose snake*

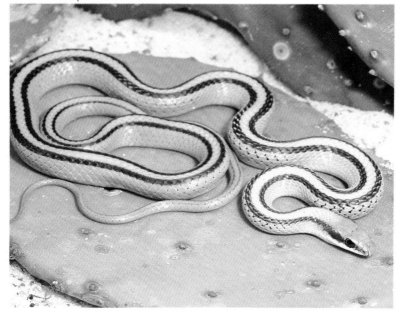

**36**  *Big Bend patchnose snake*

**37**  *Rough green snake*

**38** *Western smooth green snake*

**39** *Texas rat snake*

**39**   *Texas rat snake (juvenile)*

**40**   *Baird's rat snake*

**40**  *Baird's rat snake (juvenile)*

**41**  *Great Plains rat snake*

**41**  *Great Plains rat snake (juvenile)*

**42**  *Trans-Pecos rat snake*

2   *Trans-Pecos rat snake*

**42**   *Trans-Pecos rat snake (pale phase)*

**43**  *Prairie kingsnake*

**44**  *Eastern hognose snake*

**44**   *Eastern hognose snake*

**44**   *Eastern hognose snake (defensive tail coiling and neck swelling)*

**44**   *Eastern hognose snake (death feigning)*

**45**   *Dusty hognose snake*

**46** *Plains hognose snake*

**47** *Mexican hognose snake*

**48**  *Western hooknose snake*

**49**  *Mexican hooknose snake*

George O. Miller

0  *Bullsnake*

**51**  *Louisiana pine snake*

61

**52**  *Sonoran gopher snake*

**53**  *Texas glossy snake*

**54** *Kansas glossy snake*

**55** *Painted Desert glossy snake*

**56** *Speckled kingsnake*

**57** *Desert kingsnake*

**58**  *Eastern coachwhip*

**58**  *Eastern coachwhip (juvenile)*

**59**   *Western coachwhip*

**59**   *Western coachwhip*

9  *Western coachwhip*

9  *Western coachwhip*

**60** *Central Texas whipsnake*

**61** *Desert striped whipsnake*

**62** *Schott's whipsnake*

**63** *Ruthven's whipsnake*

**64**   *Eastern yellowbelly racer*

**64**   *Eastern yellowbelly racer (hatchling)*

**65**  *Mexican racer (juvenile)*

**66**  *Southern black racer*

**66** *Southern black racer (juvenile)*

**67** *Buttermilk racer*

72

**69** *Central American speckled racer*

**70** *Texas indigo snake*

**71** *Diamondback water snake*

**72** *Blotched water snake*

**2** *Blotched water snake (juvenile)*

**73** *Yellowbelly water snake*

**74**  *Broad-banded water snake*

**75**  *Gulf salt marsh snake*

**76**  *Florida water snake*

**77**  *Green water snake*

**78** *Brazos water snake*

**79** *Concho water snake*

**80**  *Graham's crayfish snake*

**81**  *Gulf crayfish snake*

**82**   *Western mud snake*

**82**   *Western mud snake*

*Texas night snake*

*Spotted night snake*

**85** Black-striped snake

**86** Texas lyre snake

**87**   *Northern cat-eyed snake*

*Texas longnose snake*

**89** *Louisiana milk snake*

**90** *Mexican milk snake*

*New Mexico milk snake*

**92**    *Central Plains milk snake (juvenile)*

**93** *Gray-banded kingsnake (Blair phase)*

**93** *Gray-banded kingsnake (Blair phase)*

*Gray-banded kingsnake (alterna phase)*

**94** *Northern scarlet snake*

**95**  *Texas scarlet snake*

**96**  *Texas coral snake*

**97** *Western cottonmouth*

**97** *Western cottonmouth (juvenile)*

**98**   *Southern copperhead*

**99**   *Broad-banded copperhead*

Craig McIntyre

**100**   *Trans-Pecos copperhead*

**101**   *Western diamondback rattlesnake*

91

**102** *Prairie rattlesnake*

**103** *Timber rattlesnake*

**104** *Northern blacktail rattlesnake*

**105** *Mojave rattlesnake*

**106**   *Mottled rock rattlesnake*

**106**   *Mottled rock rattlesnake*

**107** *Banded rock rattlesnake*

**108** *Western massasauga*

**109** *Desert massasauga*

**110** *Western pigmy rattlesnake*

# *LEPTOTYPHLOPIDAE*

# Plains Blind Snake

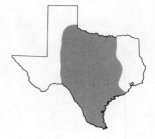

*Leptotyphlops dulcis dulcis*

**Nonvenomous**   This tiny serpent is much too small to bite humans.

**Abundance**   Common, especially in early spring before the upper layers of soil have dried and hardened with hot weather, forcing blind snakes deeper into the earth.

**Size**   Two and a half to 11 inches long, *L. d. dulcis* looks much like a large earthworm.

**Habitat**   A predominantly subterranean reptile most often found at the surface beneath leaf and plant litter or under decaying logs.

**Prey**   The eggs, larvae, and pupae of ants and termites; sometimes the adults of soft-bodied insects as well.

**Reproduction**   Egg-bearing. During late June and early July, female blind snakes sometimes deposit their clutches of up to 8 thin-shelled, ½-inch-long eggs in a communal nesting cavity hollowed out in decaying vegetation or loose, sandy soil.

**Coloring/scale form**   *Leptotyphlops'* vestigial eyes are no more than dots of dark pigment barely visible beneath its enlarged, translucent ocular scales, each of which extends to the mouth and, in the plains subspecies, is preceded by a single upper labial scale. Unlike those of other native snakes, the belly scales are not transversely widened into elongate plates (14 rows of smooth scales encircle the whole trunk), and the tail is tipped with a tiny spur.

**Similar snakes**   The **New Mexico blind snake (2)** is found west of the Cap Rock on the High Plains, where it is distinguished by the 2 upper labial scales that occur just forward of the lower portion of each ocular scale. See illustration at New Mexico blind snake.

**Behavior**   The specialized spur on blind snakes' tail tips is dug into their tunnel walls to obtain purchase in pressing ahead through the soil, while on open ground it is brought forward, planted, and used to lever the rest of the body ahead.

# New Mexico Blind Snake

*Leptotyphlops dulcis dissectus*

The New Mexico blind snake is differentiated from the Trans-Pecos blind snake (3), which shares most of its High Plains and northern Chihuahuan Desert range, by the 3 small scales—the Trans-Pecos has only 1—that separate the tops of the ocular plates on its crown. The New Mexico race is in turn distinguished from its subspecies, the plains blind snake (1), by the presence of 2 narrow upper labial scales—*dissectus* means "cleft," in reference to their shared central suture—between the lower extension of the ocular plate and the nasal scale; the plains race has but 1 such intervening scale. In other respects New Mexico blind snakes resemble the plains race, and intergrades between the 2 forms are common.

Behavior is probably identical, including the deposition of several egg clutches in the same nest cavity. Of necessity, *dissectus* burrow quite deeply to avoid desiccation in arid country; individuals have been unearthed from several feet below the surface by road-grading machinery in extremely dry, sandy terrain near Castolon on the Rio Grande.

Trans-Pecos blind snake
(L. h. segregus)

Plains and New Mexico
blind snakes
(L. dulcis)

Plains blind snake
(L. d. dulcis)

New Mexico blind snake
(L. d. dissectus)

# Trans-Pecos Blind Snake

*Leptotyphlops humilis segregus*

**Nonvenomous**   This animal is too small to bite humans.

**Abundance**   Fairly common, but so inconspicuous that they are seldom noticed, Trans-Pecos blind snakes are well dispersed over their range.

**Size**   Slightly larger than the plains and New Mexico blind snakes, *L. h. segregus* reaches a maximum length of 13 inches.

**Habitat**   A variety of biotic communities, most often grassland.

**Prey**   Principally the eggs and pupae of ants and termites.

**Reproduction**   Egg-bearing; presumably similar to the plains blind snake (1).

**Coloring/scale form**   The shiny, flesh-colored back may have a slight brown tinge on 5 to 7 of its vertebral scale rows; the belly is pale pink. Along with 95 other species and subspecies of Leptotyphlopidae (many of which are abundant in the American tropics), this little reptile has a cylindrical head and a tail of almost the same diameter as its midsection, so that both its ends look remarkably alike. The tail is given away, however, by the tiny spur at its tip and by its tendency to wriggle back and forth, smearing musky cloacal fluid over the rest of the body. This musk functions as an olfactory armor against the bites of ants, whose nests blind snakes must enter for food, enhancing the protection afforded by the tightly overlapping scales. Fourteen rows of these scales encircle the entire trunk, for the elongation of the belly scales into the transverse plates of most serpents is absent.

**Similar snakes**   Only other Leptotyphlopidae are similar. Both the **plains (1)** and the **New Mexico (2) blind snake** are distinguished by the 3 small scales present in the center of the crown between the tops of the right and left ocular plates; a single midcrown scale separates the oculars of the Trans-Pecos blind snake. See illustration at New Mexico blind snake.

**Behavior**   L. M. Klauber (Transactions of the San Diego Society of Natural History 9:163–94, 1940) writes that this little serpent "progress[es] with less lateral undulation than other snakes. On smooth surfaces it . . . employ[s] the tail spine to aid in its motion. When placed in loose or sandy soil it burrows immediately. It is never peaceful or quiet when above ground, but continually searches for something in which to burrow."

# COLUBRIDAE

# Mississippi Ringneck Snake

*Diadophis punctatus stictogenys*

**Nonvenomous**   *Diadophis punctatus* does not ordinarily bite humans, even when picked up in the field.

**Abundance**   Generally uncommon in Texas. Several individuals may share the microenvironment within a rotting log, under a large stone, or beneath discarded lumber or sheets of roofing material, however.

**Size**   Most adults are 10 to 12 inches in length.

**Habitat**   Throughout its range *D. p. stictogenys* seems to prefer damp meadow and woodland; overgrown fields near water and the litter-filled bottoms of ravines and gullies are also inhabited.

**Prey**   Earthworms, slugs, insect larvae, and very small frogs, salamanders, skinks, and hatchling snakes—which are located primarily by scent beneath woodland ground cover.

**Reproduction**   Egg-bearing. The 2 to 8 elongate, inch-long eggs are sometimes deposited in a common site (frequently within a rotting pine log) used by several females; the 4- to 5-inch young emerge in as little as 5 weeks.

**Coloring/scale form**   Usually arranged in 15 rows on the forebody, the dorsal scales are smooth; the belly, patterned with a double row of tiny black scallops along its centerline, is cream beneath the head, shading to yellow at midbody and darkening to orange-red under the tail. A loreal scale is present, and the anal plate is divided.

**Similar snakes**   A western subspecies, the **prairie ringneck (5),** is distinguished by its scattered black belly scallops as well as by its 17 forebody rows of dorsal scales. The **Texas brown (13)** and **southern redbelly (15) snakes** are brownish above and have keeled dorsal scales; they lack the ringneck's black-spotted belly, their cheeks are pale, with a dark vertical splotch, and only the very young have a light band across the nape. Juvenile **earth snakes (20–21)** may also have a dimly defined pale neck ring but are more brownish above, unmarked off-white below, and have only 5 or 6 upper labial scales.

**Behavior**   Like other *Diadophis*, the Mississippi ringneck has evolved a defensive combination of color and posture that includes hiding its head under a body coil, twisting the tail into a corkscrew to expose its bright orange-red underside, and voiding musk and feces.

# Prairie Ringneck Snake

*Diadophis punctatus arnyi*

☐ *Area of intergradation*

**Nonvenomous**  Although ringnecks do not bite humans, the saliva of all *Diadophis* is evidently toxic to their small vertebrate and insect prey.

**Abundance**  Over most of the southern part of its Texas range, *D. p. arnyi* is uncommon, though in the cedar brakes of Kerr, Bandera, and Medina counties it may be somewhat more abundant, as it is in places on the High Plains.

**Size**  Usual adult length is 10 to 14 inches; the maximum recorded size is 16½ inches.

**Habitat**  Terrestrial, often subterranean. Despite its name, the prairie ringneck most often occurs in Texas beneath a sylvan canopy, yet one open enough to allow considerable sunlight to reach the ground.

**Prey**  Similar to that of the Mississippi ringneck snake (4).

**Reproduction**  Egg-bearing. See Mississippi ringneck snake (4).

**Coloring/scale form**  Separating the black head from the slate-gray back is a golden ring that in some individuals is interrupted by dark pigment over the spine. The pale gray lips, chin, and throat are speckled with black dots, while both the yellow belly and the orange-red underside of the tail are randomly marked with little black half-moons. Seventeen rows of smooth dorsal scales occur on the forebody, a loreal is present between the ocular and nasal scales, and the anal plate is divided.

**Similar snakes**  The **Mississippi ringneck (4)** has a row of paired black spots down the middle of its belly and 15 anterior rows of dorsal scales. The **regal ringneck (6),** with which the prairie race intergrades throughout West Texas, is a slightly larger, lighter gray (crown as well as back) subspecies that may entirely lack a pale neck ring; its belly color also extends a bit farther up onto its lower sides. Very young **Texas brown (13)** and **earth (20–21) snakes** may have dimly defined light-hued napes but are distinguished by their brownish backs, unmarked off-white bellies, and, except for the western smooth earth, at least faintly keeled dorsal scales.

**Behavior**  Prairie ringnecks marked during field studies are typically recaptured (a year or more later) so close to the same place that this animal's usual range is probably no more than 400 feet in diameter; travel beyond this distance ordinarily represents either a shift of the home territory or a seasonal migration to or from winter brumation or summer egg-laying sites.

*SMALL BURROWING SNAKES*

# Regal Ringneck Snake

*Diadophis punctatus regalis*

☐ *Area of intergradation*

**Nonvenomous**   The saliva of ringneck snakes is apparently toxic to their small prey, but when harassed by humans, even the largest individuals either play dead or evert the brightly colored undertail.

**Abundance**   Locally common throughout West Texas, *D. p. regalis* is seldom seen because it keeps to the cover of shrub or cactus roots and rock crevices.

**Size**   The regal ringneck is named for the comparatively statuesque proportions of more westerly populations; in Texas even the biggest females—the larger sex—seldom measure more than 18 inches in length.

**Habitat**   The Trans-Pecos uplands, under large rocks and fallen yucca logs, often near the scattered, seasonally filled pools and potholes of rocky streambeds.

**Prey**   *Regalis* reportedly feeds almost exclusively on reptiles, principally smaller snakes. Prey is grasped and chewed vigorously until immobilized by the salivary toxins introduced through repeated punctures of the slightly enlarged upper rear teeth.

**Reproduction**   Egg-bearing. Two to 5 leathery, oblong eggs are laid in early summer.

**Coloring/scale form**   The yellowish lower lip is marked with tiny black spots that continue rearward along the band of yellowish-orange belly pigment that extends 3 or 4 scale rows up onto the lower sides. Mostly on the foreparts, randomly placed black half-moons spot the yellow to dark gray belly; posteriorly, the underside is less heavily spotted as it darkens to red under the tail. There are usually 17 rows of smooth dorsal scales on the forebody; the anal plate is divided.

**Similar snakes**   Although it intergrades with the regal race throughout West Texas, the typical **prairie ringneck (5)** is a smaller serpent with a prominent yellow neck band and a black crown; its yellowish-orange ventral coloring does not extend as far (only 2 scale rows) up its sides as that of the regal ringneck. **Blackhead (8–11)** and **blackhood (12) snakes** have light brown backs and sides, black crowns, no loreal scale, and unspotted salmon-pink bellies.

**Behavior**   If frightened, a newly captured ringneck may hide its head between one's fingers, sometimes exuding a drop of saliva from the corners of its mouth while inverting a loop of the red undertail.

# Flathead Snake

*Tantilla gracilis*

**Nonvenomous**   This tiny reptile is unable to bite humans.

**Abundance**   Flathead snakes are among the most abundant of the small, soil-colored serpents that turn up in flower beds and gardens in the eastern two thirds of the state; several individuals may be found together in particularly favorable microhabitats such as compost heaps.

**Size**   From 3 inches and not much thicker than coathanger wire at hatching to 10 inches.

**Habitat**   *T. gracilis* prefers loose, slightly damp soil in which to burrow, and consequently occurs most often in well-watered deciduous woods and grass-brushland communities.

**Prey**   Primarily small centipedes and earth-dwelling insect larvae such as cutworms and wireworms.

**Reproduction**   Egg-bearing. Breeding takes place during the first half of May, with clutches of 1 to 4 eggs being deposited during the second 2 weeks in June; the eggs hatch after about 60 days of incubation, depending on the temperature.

**Coloring/scale form**   Flattened from top and bottom, the snout appears rounded from above; belly color is salmon pink. Although too small to note easily with the naked eye, there is a single postocular scale and no loreal (the second of the 6 upper labial scales touches, or almost touches, the prefrontal); the smooth dorsal scales are arranged in 15 rows at midbody and the anal plate is divided.

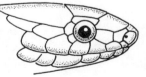

*Earth snake*

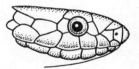

*Flathead snake*

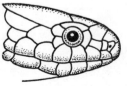

*Ground snake*

*SMALL BURROWING SNAKES*

**Similar snakes**   The **plains blackhead snake (8)** has 7 upper labial scales, a sharply defined black skullcap that stretches back 3 to 5 scale rows behind its crown to terminate in a point on the nape, and a whitish-edged pink belly. The **earth snakes (20–21)** have a loreal scale and 17 rows of dorsal scales, with faint keels on those of at least the middorsal rows. (The rough earth snake also has 5 upper labial scales and more grayish coloration.) The **ground snake (19)** is paler, and those living in the flathead's range usually have a yellowish or reddish-tan ground color, as well as an often crossbanded back and undertail; it has both a loreal and paired postocular scales.

**Behavior**   Shy and largely nocturnal, *T. gracilis* is active mainly between April and early November, withdrawing well below ground during the winter by insinuating itself through tiny crevices in the earth.

# Plains Blackhead Snake

*Tantilla nigriceps fumiceps*

**Nonvenomous**   This docile little reptile is unable to bite people.

**Abundance**   Moderately abundant in places such as the thorn brush of the Rio Grande plain and the shortgrass prairie of the Panhandle.

**Size**   Adults are 7 to 14-3/4 inches in length.

**Habitat**   Loose, often slightly damp soil under rocks and debris, most often in open grassland or thorn brush savannah.

**Prey**   Primarily centipedes, worms, spiders, insects, and insect larvae taken in semisubterranean locations.

**Reproduction**   Egg-bearing. See flathead snake (7).

**Coloring/scale form**   The plains blackhead's black skullcap is longer than those of other *Tantilla*, stretching back 3 to 5 vertebral scale rows to end in a point on the nape; there is a ruddy flush along the midbelly. Arranged in 15 rows at midbody, the dorsal scales are smooth; there is a single postocular and 7 upper labial scales, the second of which, due to the absence of a loreal, touches the prefrontal plate that caps the snout just ahead of the eye. The anterior lower labials generally touch beneath the chin (see illustration), and the anal plate is divided.

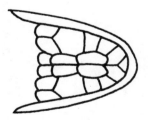
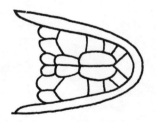

*Underchin: plains blackhead snake*    *Underchin: southwestern blackhead snake*

***Similar snakes***   The **flathead snake (7)** has 6 upper labial scales and a short brown skullcap whose slightly concave rear border extends rearward no more than 2 scale rows beyond the parietal plates of its crown. The straight rear-bordered skullcap of the Trans-Pecos' **southwestern blackhead (9)** reaches no more than a single dorsal scale row onto its nape (where it may be edged with a faint paler line), its rostral scale is a bit more pointed, and its first pair of lower labials do not touch under the chin. The **ground snake (19)** also has a loreal scale, a pair of postocular scales, a very faint light-dark pattern on each dorsal scale that gives its back a slightly textured appearance, and often a crossbanded back and undertail.

***Behavior***   In Texas, blackhead snakes are most active from March to November, although temperature and soil moisture are the major determinants of their presence at the surface. Dry summer heat can induce a period of aestivation, while low winter temperatures force these animals to withdraw as much as several feet into the ground—though warm midwinter periods may find them near the surface once more.

# Southwestern Blackhead Snake

*Tantilla hobartsmithi*

**Nonvenomous**   This little *Tantilla* never bites humans.

**Abundance**   Moderately abundant, though seldom reported because its range is sparsely populated by human beings and its inaccessible underground microenvironment usually enables it to escape their attention.

**Size**   Maximum adult length is no more than 9-1/4 inches.

**Habitat**   A burrowing animal ordinarily found on the surface only where moisture has condensed under flat stones or litter.

**Prey**   The stomachs of 37 individuals contained only butterfly, moth, and beetle larvae even though many other small animals were available in the immediate vicinity.

**Reproduction**   Egg-bearing. One Big Bend female carrying a single egg ready to be laid was discovered on the first of June; little else is known.

**Coloring/scale form**   An orangish streak lines the center of the forebelly; posteriorly the entire belly is salmon. The black cap—along whose straight or slightly convex rear border a thin pale wash sometimes occurs—is smaller than that of other *Tantilla*, barely reaching beyond the posterior edge of the parietal scales and extending no farther down the cheeks than a horizontal line through the middle of the 7 upper labial scales. The 15 midbody rows of dorsal scales are smooth and the anterior lower labials usually do not meet beneath the chin (see illustration at plains blackhead [8]). There is no loreal scale, and the anal plate is divided.

**Similar snakes**   The black skullcap of the **plains blackhead snake (8)** tapers rearward along the nape to a point 3 to 5 scale rows behind the parietal plates, and the first pair of labial scales meets under the chin; the **flathead snake (7)** has a brown skullcap with a slightly concave rear border and 6 upper labial scales. The **ground snake (19)** has a loreal scale, there are 2 postoculars, and the belly is off-white except for the pattern of transverse dark stripes that is sometimes found under the tail.

**Behavior**   In spring and summer this animal is usually confined at the surface to the shadiest, dampest microhabitats beneath rocks; where it lives below ground during the rest of the year is not known.

*SMALL BURROWING SNAKES*

# Mexican Blackhead Snake

*Tantilla atriceps*

Basing their studies primarily on the spinal morphology of their subjects' hemipenes, Charles Cole and Laurence Hardy have revised the classification of the animal formerly known as the Mexican blackhead snake into 2 separate species. Writing in the *Bulletin of the American Museum of Natural History* (vol. 171, 1981), these authors define *Tantilla hobartsmithi* as the southwestern blackhead (9), with a range that includes all of the state west and northwest of Kinney, Edwards, and Sutton counties. The old Latin designation, *Tantilla atriceps*— which formerly applied to the West Texas blackhead population as well—has now been assigned to a very rare serpent so far found north of the Rio Grande only in Duval County. Almost nothing is known about its natural history, but because of its predominantly Tamaulipan range, it has been given the common name of Mexican blackhead.

# Devil's River Blackhead Snake

*Tantilla rubra diabola*

**Nonvenomous**   *Rubra* is the only *Tantilla* that is large and assertive enough to nip a human assailant.

**Abundance**   Rare; only a few dozen specimens are recorded, although as many as 8 individuals have been found in a single area within a few days' time when weather and soil conditions were optimal.

**Size**   Moderately sizable compared to other *Tantilla:* examples have measured between 8½ and 15 inches in length.

**Habitat**   Devil's River blackheads are found in both broken and flat terrain throughout Terrell and Val Verde counties.

**Prey**   Apparently almost exclusively centipedes.

**Reproduction**   Egg-bearing. Two or 3 slender, inch-long whitish eggs are deposited once a year; one captive female laid such a clutch on June 13, 1983.

**Coloring/scale form**   *T. r. diabola*'s most distinctive marking is its black head and anterior neck, broken by a prominent white collar. The snout is often tipped with white, an oval or irregularly shaped white spot is usually present on the upper lip just below and behind the eye (a few pale specks may also dot the forwardmost upper labial scales), and the belly is off-white. Arranged in 15 rows at midbody, the dorsal scales are smooth; the anal plate is divided.

**Similar snakes**   The dark crown of the **plains blackhead snake (8)** is pointed or convex along its rear edge, is not followed by a light collar, and does not extend onto the lower jaw, while the **southwestern blackhead (9)** has an abbreviated dark skullcap that extends laterally only as far as the middle of its upper labial scales; its lower labials and chin are whitish. Although a narrow pale line is occasionally evident just behind the black cap, this area is never followed by a black band. Both these animals also have pinkish bellies. The **regal ringneck snake (6)** has a slate-gray back and a black-spotted orange belly.

**Behavior**   *Rubra diabola*'s sporadic forays above ground occur mostly during June and July and are almost always associated with precipitation: each of 6 individuals found on the pavement, as well as 2 specimens collected in the field, turned up following rainy periods.

*SMALL BURROWING SNAKES*

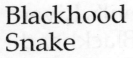

# Blackhood Snake

*Tantilla rubra cucullata*

**Nonvenomous**   Shy, secretive, and nonaggressive.

**Abundance**   Very rare. Known from fewer than 30 specimens, this burrowing serpent seldom emerges from its subterranean microenvironment within the Trans-Pecos uplands.

**Size**   The few recorded blackhood snakes have measured between 8½ and 17¼ inches in length.

**Habitat**   Known only from elevations between 1,300 and 5,000 feet in the Chisos and Davis mountains.

**Prey**   On the basis of the feeding behavior of captives, the diet is evidently limited to arthropods and annelids, especially small centipedes and slugs.

**Reproduction**   Egg-bearing. See Devil's River blackhead snake (11).

**Coloring/scale form**   Similar in most respects to the subspecies Devil's River blackhead, the blackhood has two distinctly different nuchal-cephalic patterns. In one, except for some pale spots on the lower jaw, the head and neck are wrapped in a solid black hood; in the other, the dark hood is interrupted across the nape by a light collar split with blackish pigment over the spine, the tip of the snout bears a white spot, and white dots occur on the upper labial scales both ahead of and behind the eye. Although both color phases are found together in Big Bend, they are largely geographically separated, for 10 of 18 *cucullata* reported from the Chisos Mountains were the light-collared variety, while those from northern Brewster, Jeff Davis, and Presidio counties are usually solid-hood morphs. Both phases have whitish bellies, and like those of all *Tantilla*, the smooth dorsal scales are arranged in 15 rows at midbody; the anal plate is divided.

**Similar snakes**   The **Devil's River blackhead (11)** has an uninterrupted pale neck ring and fewer white facial markings. The black cap of the **plains blackhead (8)** does not include the lower jaw, and there is never a light collar across the nape. The abbreviated dark skullcap of the **southwestern blackhead (9)** extends rearward no more than a single scale row beyond the parietal scales of its crown; laterally, this marking does not reach below the mouth. Both plains and southwestern blackheads also have pinkish bellies.

**Behavior**   Little known, but probably much the same as that of the Devil's River blackhead (11).

# Texas Brown Snake

*Storeria dekayi texana*

**Nonvenomous**   Does not bite when handled.

**Abundance**   Very common.

**Size**   Adults average 9½ to 12 inches in length; recorded to 18 inches.

**Habitat**   Brown snakes are burrowers partial to the moist conditions often found beneath flat stones, as well as within the porous undersides of decaying trunks, branches, and other woody debris. In Texas, macrohabitat includes both the riparian bottomland of hill country oak-juniper brakes and the overgrown pastures and open deciduous woodland of the Cross Timbers.

**Prey**   In addition to the natural shelter of rocks and logs, the fallen planks and sheets of corrugated iron that litter abandoned farms shelter a host of arthropods, annelids, and larval insects, which constitute food for the brown, lined, ringneck, flathead, and earth snakes that also inhabit this spacious microenvironment.

**Reproduction**   Live-bearing, with most births occurring between the middle of June and the first week in August. Litters contain 3 to 27 young, 3½ to 4½ inches long, with solid gray-brown backs and sides and a pale band across the napes of their necks.

**Coloring/scale form**   Reddish brown to yellowish tan above, Texas brown snakes have prominent white cheeks, which directly below the eye are blotched by a pronounced brown spot; another brown mark occupies the side of the pale neck. The yellowish- or very faintly pinkish-white belly is unmarked except for black dots along its sides. There are 17 midbody rows of strongly keeled dorsal scales, no loreal scale, and a divided anal plate.

**Similar snakes**   The subspecies **marsh brown snake (14)** is distinguished by a dark little horizontal bar that lines its light-hued temporal and postocular scales, as well as by the light color and lack of markings of both the suboculars and the sixth and seventh upper labial scales; see illustration at marsh brown snake. **Southern redbelly snakes (15)** have 15 dorsal scale rows, pale areas on their napes, and red to ocher to blue-black bellies. Juvenile Texas browns, whose pale collars cause them to resemble young **Mississippi (4)** and **prairie (5) ringneck snakes,** can be differentiated from *Diadophis* by their keeled scales, off-white bellies and undertails, and light-colored cheeks.

**Behavior**   When frightened, some Texas brown snakes engage in the unusual threat gesture of partially baring their front teeth and laterally flattening their necks.

*SMALL BURROWING SNAKES*

# Marsh Brown Snake

*Storeria dekayi limnetes*

Along a 60- to 80-mile-wide strip of the upper coastal plain just inland from the Gulf, the Texas brown snake is replaced by its subspecies, the marsh brown. In this predominantly prairie community, *S. d. limnetes* hides in grassy hummocks or, when the rice fields are flooded during spring and fall growing seasons, retreats to the irrigation levees that protrude a foot or two above these artificial lakes. Marsh browns are also found among the high-tide flotsam of the coastal barrier islands—the type specimen from which this subspecies' description is drawn was collected under such driftwood—while on Galveston Island this is the predominant small "garden snake" occurring around houses.

Sometimes called DeKay's snakes, both the marsh and the Texas brown *Storeria* are named for James Ellsworth DeKay, who in the early nineteenth century first recorded the northern race on the middle Atlantic seaboard. The subspecies designation *limnetes* refers to the slim horizontal bar marking the temporal and postocular scales, which, along with the unmarked upper and lower labial scales, differentiates this race from *S. d. texana*. Its prey (mostly earthworms), reproduction, and natural history are probably identical to the Texas brown snake's.

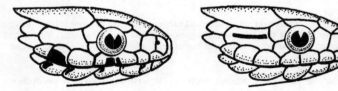

*Texas brown snake*      *Marsh brown snake*

# Southern Redbelly Snake

*Storeria occipitomaculata obscura*

***Nonvenomous*** Like its brown snake relatives, *S. o. obscura* is a shy little woodland animal that never bites humans.

***Abundance*** Rare in Texas, and restricted in range, having been recorded only in Anderson, Bowie, Hardin, Harrison, Houston, Jefferson, Orange, San Jacinto, Smith, and Wood counties.

***Size*** Average adult length is 8 to 10 inches, with a maximum size of 16 inches.

***Habitat*** *S. o. obscura* occurs sporadically in moist, forested parts of East Texas, where it apparently lives mainly beneath decaying logs.

***Prey*** Slugs seem to be the primary prey, but earthworms are probably also taken.

***Reproduction*** Live-bearing; the young, 2¾ to 4 inches long and numbering up to 23 per litter, are born between June and September. Grayer than adults and usually lacking their dark dorsal spots, neonates are patterned with a pale band across the nape.

***Coloring/scale form*** Several Anderson County individuals were uniformly yellowish brown above, with yellow bellies, but the 3 characteristic light spots behind the head were barely discernible: the only markings on the back were a faint row of dark dots on either side of the spine. The prominent white spot under the eye to which this species' Latin name refers was present, but there was no black border below it. Another individual, found on the southwest edge of Beaumont, had a solid dark brown back and blackish lower sides whose color extended onto the outer edges of its reddish-orange ventral scales—a pattern similar to that of a brown-bellied Bowie County specimen that also had no black border below its white subocular spot. *S. o. obscura*'s keeled dorsal scales occur in 15 midbody rows, there is no loreal scale (though a postnasal scale touches the preocular), and the anal plate is divided.

***Similar snakes*** The **Texas brown snake (13)** has a dark subocular spot, while the **marsh brown (14)** has a dark horizontal line behind its eye; both have pale cheeks and 17 rows of dorsal scales at midbody.

***Behavior*** Harmless to larger animals, the southern redbelly relies for defense on an injury-and-death-feigning display: after rolling over, mouth agape and tongue hanging loosely, it may flatten the body laterally in several places as though injured.

*SMALL BURROWING SNAKES*

# Texas Lined Snake

*Tropidoclonion lineatum texanum*

☐ *Area of intergradation*

**Nonvenomous**   Lined snakes do not bite human beings, although if molested, a large specimen may flatten the neck and engage in bluffing strikes.

**Abundance**   Throughout both the central prairie and the eastern Edwards Plateau oak-juniper savannah, *T. l. texanum* is locally common, often in areas of altered and softened soil near rural houses.

**Size**   Most adults measure between 8 and 12 inches in length. Among the intergrade (with the more northerly central race, *T. l. annectens*) population living in the Fort Worth–Dallas area, J. P. Jones, former reptile director of the Fort Worth Zoo, recorded one gravid Tarrant County female of 21½ inches, while Dallas Zoo director Jack Joy reports having seen specimens at least an inch longer in Dallas County.

**Habitat**   Principally a grassland animal most often found under rocks on open prairie, as well as along pasture-woodland interface.

**Prey**   Primarily earthworms. *T. l. texanum* is also one of the few vertebrates to feed occasionally on toxic sow bugs.

**Reproduction**   Live-bearing; 23 Oklahoma broods of the 4- to 5-inch-long newborns were deposited between August 9 and August 31.

**Coloring/scale form**   A slender little serpent whose pointed head, no wider than its neck, is adapted for burrowing. The throat and belly are ordinarily creamy (though the midventral region may have a dull yellowish cast) with a double row of rearward-arched small black half-moons. The keeled dorsal scales occur in 19 rows at midbody, 17 rows just anterior to the vent. There are 143 or fewer ventral scales, usually 6 (sometimes 5) upper labial scales, and the anal plate is undivided.

**Similar snakes**   Only the **central lined snake (17)** is very similar (see central lined snake). **Garter snakes (23–29)** have dark-checkered backs, heads twice the width of their necks when seen from above, and 8 upper labial scales vertically edged with black along their sutures; none has a double row of black ventral half-moons.

**Behavior**   Lined snakes are seldom seen in the open, typically remaining coiled beneath cover during the day.

# Central Lined Snake

☐ *Area of intergradation*   *Tropidoclonion lineatum annectens*

In a wide band stretching from North Central Texas across Oklahoma into Kansas, the Texas lined snake intergrades with its very similar northern subspecies, the central lined race, *T. l. annectens,* first defined by L. W. Ramsey in 1953. This form is differentiated only by its larger total number of ventral scales: 144 or more.

*SMALL BURROWING SNAKES*

# New Mexico Lined Snake

*Tropidoclonion lineatum mertensi*

Donald Tinkle and G. N. Knopf (Herpetologica 20:42–47, 1964) reported lined snakes from the extreme northwestern Panhandle that were probably members of the New Mexico subspecies, *T. l. mertensi,* named for German herpetologist Robert Mertens. These grassland reptiles are typically found under flat rocks or dried dung and differ from the Texas and central races only in scalation: the New Mexico form has 5 upper labial scales, 16 dorsal scale rows just ahead of the vent (17 for the Texas and central races), and 17 or 18 scale rows at midbody (19 for the Texas and central races).

# Ground Snake

*Sonora semiannulata*

**Nonvenomous**   Does not bite humans.

**Abundance**   Widely distributed over all but the eastern quarter of the state, and often locally common, especially in oak-juniper savannah.

**Size**   Usually less than a foot in length; the record is 16⅜ inches.

**Habitat**   Almost every well-vegetated terrestrial milieu in the western two thirds of the state; in suburban areas ground snakes are usually associated with disturbed habitat such as dumps or vacant lots where debris is piled.

**Prey**   Primarily centipedes, scorpions, and spiders.

**Reproduction**   Egg-bearing. Most of the Texas population lay their clutches (averaging 4.1 eggs) during the first week of June.

**Coloring/scale form**   *S. semiannulata* is characterized by an array of colors and patterns—of which several different combinations may be found even among a small group living in a single rock pile. Generally, however, specimens from Central Texas are unmarked yellowish tan above (sometimes with a small dark band across the nape), while just west of the hill country ground snakes exhibit up to 35 dark brown or black dorsal or dorsolateral crossbars that may completely encircle the tail. Trans-Pecos individuals are typically more brightly colored, often having an orange-red vertebral stripe sometimes broken by short black crossbars. Their lower sides are usually a lighter pinkish or yellowish tan, sometimes with tiny rectangular blocks or checkers forming a dashed lateral line; other individuals from this region are entirely salmon-hued above. All *Sonora* have light bellies, usually without markings forward of the vent, as well as 13 to 15 midbody rows of very slightly darker-centered smooth dorsal scales—scalation that gives ground snakes' backs a faintly woven-textured appearance not present on other small serpents. The head is blunt, rounded, and only a bit wider than the neck, with a loreal scale that does not touch the eye, 2 postoculars, and either 6 or 7 upper labials; the anal plate is divided.

**Similar snakes**   **Flathead (7)** and **blackhead (8–11) snakes** lack a loreal scale and have proportionately smaller, ventrodorsally flattened brown- or black-crowned heads, unmarked backs with no light-dark scale patterning, and salmon-colored midbellies. **Earth snakes (20–21)** have 17 rows of dorsal scales that lack the ground snake's faintly two-toned pigmentation (the smooth earth is uniformly reddish tan above, the rough earth solid gray-brown; unmarked ground snakes are usually yellowish), and the loreal touches the eye.

*SMALL BURROWING SNAKES*

**Behavior**  Shy and secretive, ground snakes are primarily nocturnal, spending most of their lives within burrows or stony crevices and venturing abroad only at night, usually during damp weather. Their predators include larger snakes, armadillos, skunks, and, in South Texas, javelinas. Some *S. semiannulata* exhibit the same head-hiding, tail-waving defensive response as the similarly undertail-banded coral snake.

# Western Smooth Earth Snake

*Virginia valeriae elegans*

**Nonvenomous**   Too small to bite humans.

**Abundance**   In the meadows of the eastern Edwards Plateau's cedar brakes *Virginia valeriae elegans* is locally abundant.

**Size**   Adults measure 7 to 13 inches in length.

**Habitat**   Microhabitat is generally beneath flat rocks, logs, and boards on partially wooded rural hillsides, as well as in densely vegetated (usually oak-juniper) suburban residential neighborhoods.

**Prey**   Mainly earthworms.

**Reproduction**   Live-bearing. One 11½-inch-long reddish-tan North Texas female gave birth on August 20 to seven 4-inch charcoal-gray neonates.

**Coloring/scale form**   The belly is unmarked white, sometimes with a yellowish wash; the 17 midbody rows of dorsal scales are predominantly smooth, though faint keels may appear along the spine on the posterior portion of the back. (Dark hairline seams that resemble keels also mark the centers of a number of adjacent scales.) The forward edge of the eye is touched by a horizontally lengthened loreal scale, while a pair of small postoculars borders the rear of the eye (see illustration). There are usually 6 upper labials, and the anal plate is divided.

*Ground snake*            *Flathead snake*            *Earth snake*

**Similar snakes**   The **rough earth snake (21)** is grayer and lacks a pinkish cast to its lower sides and belly. It has more distinctly keeled dorsolateral scales and 5 upper labials. The **flathead snake (7)** has a slightly slimmer, more yellowish-brown body with a flattened, chocolate-capped head, a salmon-pink belly, no loreal scale, a single postocular, and 15 rows of smooth dorsal scales. The **ground snake (19)** has 15 or fewer rows of smooth dorsal scales, a small preocular separating the eye and the loreal, and a faintly braided appearance derived from the very slightly lighter-hued borders of its dorsal scales; among western specimens the underside of the tail is also usually crossbanded.

**Behavior**   This secretive burrowing reptile seems to be most active above ground during cool early spring weather and, as late as December in Travis County, just before retiring for its winter dormancy.

*SMALL BURROWING SNAKES*

# Rough Earth Snake

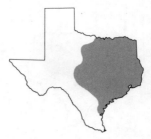

*Virginia striatula*

**Nonvenomous**   This animal is not big enough to bite humans.

**Abundance**   The most common serpent in most of the long strip of inter-mingled oak-hickory woodland and blackland prairie that stretches north-ward from the coastal plain into Oklahoma.

**Size**   Up to 12½ inches in length, with a diameter usually less than that of a pencil.

**Habitat**   The little burrowing snake typically seen beneath boards and fallen siding around abandoned farms, *Virginia striatula* is most evident at the sur-face when the soil is moist from recent rains.

**Prey**   The stomachs of one sample of 45 *V. striatula* contained only earthworms.

**Reproduction**   Live-bearing. Sixteen litters ranged in number from 3 to 8 young measuring 3 to 4½ inches in length, with a pale band across the back of the head and the nape.

**Coloring/scale form**   Unmarked grayish brown above, with slightly darker pigmentation around the eyes and on the upper labial scales. Several of the 17 midbody rows of dorsal scales are slightly keeled, the belly is cream in color, a horizontally elongate loreal scale touches the front of the eye, and there are 2 small postoculars, usually 5 upper labial scales, and (almost al-ways) a divided anal plate.

**Similar snakes**   Most similar is the **western smooth earth snake (20),** which is distinguished by its reddish-brown color, its usual 6 upper labials, and its smoother dorsal scales. **Flathead snakes (7)** have ventrodorsally compressed dark-crowned heads, tan backs and sides, pink bellies, no loreal, a single postocular, and smooth dorsal scales. **Ground snakes (19)** are distinguished by their 15 or fewer rows of smooth dorsal scales (whose very faintly textured appearance results from these scales' slightly lighter edges and darker cen-ters); the loreal does not touch the eye. Like newborn earth snakes, hatchling **ringneck snakes (4–5)** are marked with a pale band across the rear of the skull but have smooth dorsal scales and black-speckled yellow or orange bellies.

**Behavior**   Although its lightly shielded head is less effective in rooting through rocky ground than the hooked or armored snouts of larger burrow-ing serpents, *Virginia striatula*'s pointed skull is evidently adequate for pen-etrating the moist loam where its annelid prey is most plentiful.

# Western Worm Snake

*Carphophis amoenus vermis*

**Nonvenomous**  The western worm snake is completely harmless to humans.

**Abundance**  Known only from Bowie, Red River, and Titus counties in northeastern Texas, *C. a. vermis* is one of the state's rarest serpents.

**Size**  Adults are ordinarily 7½ to 11 inches long.

**Habitat**  As a western race of an essentially eastern forest serpent, *C. a. vermis* is restricted to comparatively damp areas similar to the species' primary woodland habitat of forested stream bank, brushy meadow, and overgrown farmland.

**Prey**  Primarily earthworms, grubs, and other soft-bodied invertebrates.

**Reproduction**  Egg-bearing. In late summer, after about 7 weeks' incubation, the 1 to 8 whitish eggs, which measure 1¼ inches by ⅝ inch, hatch into 3- to 4-inch-long young.

**Coloring/scale form**  *C. a. vermis'* diminutive head, no wider than the neck, its striking dorsal and lateral coloration, and its glossy scalation are typical of a number of semisubterranean serpents such as milk, king, coral, and ringneck snakes. A distinct longitudinal demarcation separates the salmon-hued belly and lower sides from the iridescent purplish-black back. The smooth dorsal scales are arranged in only 13 midbody rows; the anal plate is divided.

**Similar snakes**  None; this is the only small burrowing snake in Texas with a bold black-and-salmon horizontal split in pigmentation along its sides.

**Behavior**  *C. a. vermis* employs a two-part defensive strategy that works very well, at least with human captors. When frightened, it expels a thick, yellowish musk from the anal glands at the base of its tail, spreading the unpleasant-smelling mucus about in its struggle to escape. In addition, in attempting to thrust itself forward, it may suddenly press its hard, pointed tail tip against a tender part of its captor's hand, producing a startling sensation so much like the prick of a tooth that one's reflexive response is to drop the animal instantly.

*SMALL BURROWING SNAKES*

# Eastern Garter Snake

*Thamnophis sirtalis sirtalis*

**Nonvenomous**   Individuals from southeastern Texas seldom bite if handled gently.

**Abundance**   Uncommon in Texas, though still observed periodically in Harris County.

**Size**   Average adult length is 18 to 26 inches, with a maximum size in Texas of 32½ inches.

**Habitat**   Primarily open or semi-open marshy lowlands: permanently wet meadows, stream banks, and ditches containing water.

**Prey**   A majority of the diet consists of earthworms, frogs, toads, and salamanders.

**Reproduction**   Live-bearing. Litters range from 7 to as many as 80, with birth occurring from early June until August; the newborns are 5 to 9 inches in length.

**Coloring/scale form**   Variable in both color and pattern, though a distinct light yellow, brownish, or greenish vertebral stripe is always evident; a similar-colored lateral seam occupies the second and third scale rows above the pale belly. (Unlike eastern garters found in other parts of the country, most individuals found along the upper Gulf Coast have red markings amid the dark pigment separating their straw-colored vertebral and lateral stripes.) Occurring in 19 rows at midbody, the dorsal scales are keeled; the anal plate is undivided.

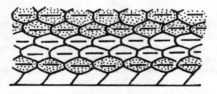

*Lateral stripe marking: eastern garter snake*

*Similar snakes*   **Western (30)** and **Gulf Coast (32) ribbon snakes** are slimmer, have proportionately longer tails, and lack both the eastern garter's dark dorsolateral spots and its vertical black labial scale sutures. The **checkered garter snake (27)** usually has 21 rows of dorsal scales and a distinctive pale yellow crescent behind the jaw that separates its black neck patch from the rearmost of its olive upper labial scales; there is no red coloring between the double row of black squares lining each side of its back.

*Behavior*   *T. s. sirtalis* is a slow, erratic forager that frequently changes direction after hesitating with its head raised for a better view. Individual ranges are usually restricted to about 2 acres, with the activity areas measured in one 3-year study averaging 600 by 150 feet; the greatest distance traveled by any of the project's subject snakes was less than ⅙ mile.

# Texas
# Garter
# Snake

*Thamnophis sirtalis annectans*

**Nonvenomous**   When picked up, Texas garters generally choose to emit musk and bump aggressively with the snout rather than bite; a large one can nip painfully, however.

**Abundance**   Fairly common in a few locales, throughout most of its East Central Texas range this reptile is seldom encountered.

**Size**   Adults average 18 to 30 inches.

**Habitat**   Marshy, flooded pastureland or meadows, particularly in spring when these areas are full of cricket and chorus frogs. At other times, Texas garter snakes are found in grassy or brushy cover near ponds and streams, including the riparian canyon habitat at the eastern edge of the Edwards Plateau.

**Prey**   Mostly earthworms, frogs, and small toads.

**Reproduction**   Live-bearing. See eastern garter snake (23).

**Coloring/scale form**   With its dark back split by a broad orange stripe that occupies the vertebral scale row as well as more than half of each adjacent row, *T. s. annectans* is a visually striking reptile. On the forward third of its trunk, the yellowish lateral stripe occupies most of the second, all of the third, and most of the fourth scale row above the belly, which is whitish or light green. Arranged in 19 rows at midbody, the dorsal scales are strongly keeled; the anal plate is undivided.

**Similar snakes**   Among Texas' garter snakes, only *T. s. annectans* has pale side stripes that involve the second, third, and fourth lateral scale rows: in the **eastern (23), New Mexico (25), checkered (27),** and **blackneck (28–29)** **garter snakes**, these stripes never occupy the fourth scale row above the belly, while the pale lateral stripe of the slenderer and longer-tailed **western ribbon snake (30)** does not occupy the second row. (Unlike those of the garters, ribbon snakes' labial scale sutures are not seamed with black, and there are no distinctly defined dark spots between their pale vertebral and lateral stripes.)

**Behavior**   Because of its active diurnal foraging, *T. s. annectans* is an interesting animal to watch. One individual came regularly to scour a small hill country pool for prey, then, after a 10-minute reconnoiter, slid away through the cedar brakes toward the Pedernales River canyon, ⅛ mile distant. This not quite 2-foot-long serpent showed no hesitation in attacking anurans much too large for it to swallow and once hung on to an adult leopard frog for 20 minutes, never managing to engulf more than a single hind leg.

# New Mexico Garter Snake

*Thamnophis sirtalis dorsalis*

***Nonvenomous***   Like most garter snakes, a large individual can deliver a sharp nip if picked up too roughly.

***Abundance***   Known in Texas solely in the El Paso area, where it is very uncommon.

***Size***   Adults ordinarily measure 18 to 28 inches in length.

***Habitat***   Only the southernmost tip of *T. s. dorsalis'* upper Rio Grande Valley range extends into Texas' El Paso County, where this snake occurs along creekbeds in both the Franklin Mountains and Fort Bliss' Castner Range, in Tom Mays and McKelligon Canyon parks, and in suburban residential neighborhoods on the northwest side of El Paso.

***Prey***   Small vertebrate or invertebrate animals.

***Reproduction***   Live-bearing. See eastern garter snake (23).

***Coloring/scale form***   The pale yellow (anteriorly) to light gray (posteriorly) line that traces the spine has a narrow black border that shades into reddish dorsolateral areas blotched with a central row of large black spots. (The red is mostly confined to the skin tucked between the predominantly dark dorsal scales.) Lower on the sides, a faint golden-tan stripe occupies the second and third scale rows above the belly, the outer edges of whose light brown or bluish scales are tipped with small black spots; the 19 midbody rows of dorsal scales are strongly keeled, and the anal plate is undivided.

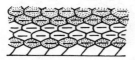

*Lateral stripe marking: New Mexico garter snake*

***Similar snakes***   There is no red on the back of the **checkered garter snake (27),** which is further distinguished by the yellow crescent followed by a large black spot located directly behind the jaw, as well as by its more whitish belly and 21 rows of dorsal scales. Another occasionally noted resident of the El Paso area, the **western blackneck garter (29),** has an even larger black blotch on each side of its neck, a pale orange vertebral stripe, and no red dorsolateral coloring.

***Behavior***   When confronted with danger, this normally somber-looking serpent may radically alter its appearance by inflating its lungs to spread its ribs and splay its dorsal scales, thus revealing the previously inconspicuous red skin.

*GARTER AND RIBBON SNAKES*

# Western Plains Garter Snake

*Thamnophis radix haydenii*

**Nonvenomous**   This animal will not bite unless handled, when it may snap abruptly in its own defense.

**Abundance**   Throughout much of its predominantly midwestern territory, *T. r. haydenii* is locally abundant, though records for Texas are sparse.

**Size**   Adults average 20 to 28 inches; the maximum recorded length is 40 inches.

**Habitat**   This subspecies' popular name suggests its prairie range, though its microenvironment is most likely to involve the borders of streams, washes, and gullies that bisect the plains.

**Prey**   Amphibians, insects (especially grasshoppers), and, among the young, earthworms.

**Reproduction**   Live-bearing, with an average of about 29 offspring per litter.

**Coloring/scale form**   The western plains garter's pale yellow side stripe occupies only the third and fourth scale rows above its belly, below which dark spots appear. (The off-white to pale greenish belly scales may also bear a line of dark distal spots.) With a maximum of 21 well-keeled rows, *T. r. haydenii* has more numerous dorsal scales than any other garter but the checkered; its anal plate is undivided.

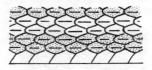

*Lateral stripe marking: western plains garter snake*

**Similar snakes**   This is a difficult snake to distinguish from the **checkered garter (27)**, whose light yellow, posteriorly black-bordered neck crescent is a bit more prominently defined, and whose light side stripe never reaches the fourth scale row above its belly line. **Ribbon snakes (30–33)** are slenderer, with proportionately longer tails, dark, unspotted backs, 19 rows of dorsal scales, and unmarked whitish lips and bellies.

**Behavior**   Normally active from March to November, western plains garter snakes are quite sensitive to high temperatures, becoming overheated at more than 90 degrees Fahrenheit. This species is relatively hardy in cool weather, though, for on sunny autumn days too chilly for most reptiles to be abroad, numbers of *T. r. haydenii* sometimes crawl onto asphalt roads to absorb warmth from the blacktop.

# Checkered Garter Snake

*Thamnophis marcianus marcianus*

**Nonvenomous**   Large checkered garters may nip if handled roughly.

**Abundance**   By far the most common terrestrial serpent in much of the southern part of the state, especially during late spring and early summer.

**Size**   Adults average 15 to 28 inches in length, with the record specimen measuring 42½ inches.

**Habitat**   In Central and North Texas *T. m. marcianus* seems to prefer grassy upland areas near water; checkered garters are much more common, however, in the thorn brush thicket of the lower coastal plain.

**Prey**   Primarily worms, tadpoles, and frogs; *T. m. marcianus* is also among the handful of serpents that sometimes feed on small carrion.

**Reproduction**   Live-bearing, with the developing young partially nourished through their mother's placenta. Birth occurs between late May and October, with 38 newborns averaging 7.8 inches in length.

**Coloring/scale form**   Most distinctive is the pale yellowish crescent behind the jaw, posteriorly bordered by a large black spot on the side of the neck. The light-hued side stripe occupies only the third row of scales above the belly on the foreparts but widens to include the second scale row over the rest of the body; the otherwise unmarked whitish-yellow belly scales sometimes have black-tipped edges. Arranged in 21 rows at midbody, the dorsal scales are keeled; the anal plate is undivided.

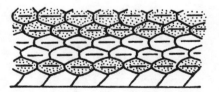

*Lateral stripe marking: checkered garter snake*

*GARTER AND RIBBON SNAKES*

***Similar snakes*** **Texas garter (24)** and **blackneck garter (28–29) snakes** lack a prominent yellow crescent behind the jaw and have only 19 midbody rows of dorsal scales. The **western plains garter (26)** has a slightly less prominent yellow nuchal crescent, while on its foreparts the pale side stripe occupies both the third and fourth scale rows above its belly. **Ribbon snakes (30–33)** are slenderer, with 19 dorsal scale rows, unspotted backs, and proportionately longer, wiry tails that make up nearly a third of their body length; unlike those of garter snakes, their white upper labial scales are not vertically marked with dark pigment.

***Behavior*** Especially abundant on warm, humid nights, checkered garters follow the typical serpentine activity pattern of foraging at dawn and dusk in spring and fall, then becoming entirely nocturnal during the heat of summer.

# Eastern
# Blackneck
# Garter Snake

*Thamnophis cyrtopsis ocellatus*

**Nonvenomous**    Eastern blacknecks generally defend themselves with only a copious discharge of feces and musk, although large individuals may nip if molested.

**Abundance**    Common: because of *T. c. ocellatus'* bright colors and diurnal foraging pattern, it is often noticed in residential neighborhoods, especially those of San Antonio, New Braunfels, San Marcos, and Austin.

**Size**    Average size is 16 to 20 inches in length; the record is 43 inches.

**Habitat**    Primarily moist, wooded ravines and streamside bottomland throughout the central hill country.

**Prey**    The eastern blackneck feeds mostly on juvenile and adult frogs and toads. Many tadpoles are taken during the spring and early summer when they are plentiful; small fish, slimy salamanders, ground skinks, red-spotted toads, and cliff frogs are sought during the rest of the year.

**Reproduction**    Live-bearing; an average brood is 9 young, 8 to 10½ inches in length.

**Coloring/scale form**    First described by C.B.R. Kennicott in 1860, the eastern blackneck takes its name from the Greek *cyrto,* "curved," and *opsis,* "appearance"—a reference to the curved black blotch located just behind its jaw. Flanking the pale orange vertebral stripe, a row of big black dorsolateral blotches encroaches downward into the forward portion of the light-hued side stripe (giving it a wavy appearance), which occupies the second and third scale rows above the belly; to the rear, these blotches diverge into a double row of staggered black spots. Arranged in 19 rows at midbody, the dorsal scales are heavily keeled; the anal plate is undivided.

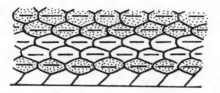

*Lateral stripe marking: eastern and western blackneck garter snakes*

*GARTER AND RIBBON SNAKES*

**Similar snakes**   No other *Thamnophis* occurring within this animal's range has a single row of very large black blotches on either side of its neck. The **redstripe ribbon snake (31)** is slenderer, with a long, wiry tail, unmarked white upper labial scales, a dull red vertebral stripe, and no dark dorsolateral spots; the pale side stripe of the **Texas garter snake (24),** unlike that of *T. c. ocellatus*, occupies part of the fourth scale row above its belly.

**Behavior**   Ironically, the blackneck's gaudy spinal pigmentation functions as sophisticated camouflage, for as the back's black spots flicker confusingly through apertures in the intervening screen of leafy undergrowth, a predator's attention tends to be focused on this seemingly stationary vertebral ribbon of orange . . . while the snake is actually rapidly sliding away.

# Western Blackneck Garter Snake

*Thamnophis cyrtopsis cyrtopsis*

**Nonvenomous**   Blackneck garters nip only if molested or handled roughly.

**Abundance**   In well-watered and -vegetated habitats, this reptile is abundant throughout Trans-Pecos Texas.

**Size**   Adults average 16 to 28 inches in length; the record is 41¾ inches.

**Habitat**   *T. c. cyrtopsis* is generally a mountain- and plateau-dweller absent from intervening low-lying valleys.

**Prey**   Mostly frogs and tadpoles.

**Reproduction**   Live-bearing; broods of 3 to 25 young have been recorded.

**Coloring/scale form**   On the forebody the pale orange vertebral stripe divides a single row of black dorsolateral squares that splits, posteriorly, into a double row. The pale side stripe occupies the second and third scale rows above the belly throughout its length, and the crown is bluish gray, strikingly set off from the big black neck patch that borders the rear of the skull; the chin and belly are white, sometimes with a faint greenish or yellowish-brown cast. Nineteen rows of keeled dorsal scales occur at midbody, and the anal plate is undivided.

**Similar snakes**   The subspecies **eastern blackneck garter (28)** has much larger, rounded or V-shaped dark anterior dorsolateral blotches, the lower tips of which reach downward into a wide yellow lateral area, giving it the configuration of a wavy stripe. Posteriorly, the black checkerboard pattern of the western race is scarcely evident. The **checkered garter (27)** is not usually found in the upland locales where the blackneck most often occurs but is distinguished by the prominent yellow crescent located just behind its jaw, by the anterior restriction of its pale side stripe to the third row of scales above its belly, and by its 21 midbody rows of dorsal scales. Found in Texas only in El Paso County, the **New Mexico garter snake (25)** lacks large black neck blotches and has both a reddish dorsal ground color and a light bluish or tan belly. **Ribbon snakes (30–33)** are slenderer, with proportionately longer tails and unmarked white upper labial scales; they also lack the garters' prominent dark neck blotch and black-blotched back.

**Behavior**   *T. cyrtopsis* is frequently encountered sunning on rocks along streambeds from which, if disturbed, it flees by swimming rapidly across the surface to the opposite bank; cornered, it may flatten its body against the ground as menacingly as possible.

*GARTER AND RIBBON SNAKES*

# Western Ribbon Snake

*Thamnophis proximus proximus*

☐ *Area of intergradation*

**Nonvenomous**   If seized roughly, despite their small heads these gracile serpents can nip and hang on tenaciously.

**Abundance**   One or another subspecies of *T. proximus* is likely to be found near any rural body of fresh water in the eastern three quarters of the state.

**Size**   Adults average 20 to 34 inches in length, with such slender bodies that 3 females (as with all *Thamnophis*, females are the larger gender) 27 to 34 inches long averaged under 6 ounces in weight.

**Habitat**   Throughout the ribbon snakes' range—from southern Wisconsin to Costa Rica—they are most often creatures of creek, lake, and pond margins; they are also found in arid brush country, though seldom far from water.

**Prey**   Seasonally variable: 92 percent of the stomach contents of one Brazos County population trapped during late spring consisted of tadpoles, but at other times of the year adult frogs and toads, lizards, and fish are the principal prey.

**Reproduction**   Live-bearing. Recorded litters have ranged from 5 to 27.

**Coloring/scale form**   Two tiny white dashes punctuate the rear of the dark crown, while the white upper labial scales are unmarked. The pale lateral stripe occupies the third and fourth scale rows above the yellowish-green belly. (The lips, light lateral stripes, and bellies of individuals living north and east of Dallas often have a bluish cast, however.) *T. p. proximus'* strongly keeled dorsal scales are arranged in 19 rows at midbody; its anal plate is undivided.

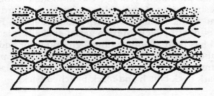

*Lateral stripe marking: ribbon snakes*

**Similar snakes**   *Thamnophis proximus'* 4 geographical races interbreed freely, producing various intermediate combinations between the **Gulf Coast ribbon (32),** which typically has a brownish- to olive-green back and sides and an olive-tan to dull gold vertebral stripe; the **redstripe ribbon (31),** which generally has a dark gray back, a wine-red vertebral stripe, and gray-green lower sides; and the **arid land ribbon (33),** whose orange vertebral stripe bisects an olive-brown to gray back and tan lower sides. **Garter snakes (23–29)** have stockier heads and bodies, shorter tails, and vertically black-lined seams between their upper labial scales. The **Texas patchnose snake (34)** has 17 rows of smooth dorsal scales, a squared-off snout capped with a big flat rostral scale, and a divided anal plate.

**Behavior**   Diurnal foragers along the shores of lakes and streams, ribbon snakes are in heavily vegetated areas sometimes partially arboreal: Collin County juveniles were observed basking in the branches of a brush-filled gully. Ribbon snakes are preyed upon by serpents such as racers and coachwhips, as well as by mammals and carnivorous birds. *Thamnophis'* conspicuous stripes may help it evade some of the latter, however, for in thick vegetation its bright undulating lines appear to converge gradually as the snake slides deeper into the bushes, leaving such a sight-hunter looking at nothing when the tail tip slips from view. So many predators thus manage to catch only this fragile caudal section—which is easily twisted off—that nearly 20 percent of the *Thamnophis* in one Kansas study lacked complete tails.

# Redstripe Ribbon Snake

*Thamnophis proximus rubrilineatus*

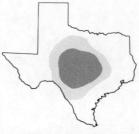

☐ *Area of intergradation*

The narrow vertebral stripe splitting the dark gray back of this subspecies can vary from deep wine red near the tail to bright orange at the nape, although entirely orange-striped specimens not infrequently turn up throughout *rubrilineatus'* range. Confined mainly to the Edwards Plateau, where it is most often found near water, the redstripe ribbon is easily observed because of its diurnal activity pattern; even when not foraging, it basks on rocks, logs, and the raised cypress knees that occur along small creeks in this region. Such individuals typically remain motionless until approached very closely, or even touched, when they streak away across the water to hide beneath overhanging rocks or vegetation on the opposite bank. During late August and September newborn ribbon snakes can often be found sheltering under creekside limestone flags.

Size, scalation, reproduction, and behavior are similar to that of the western ribbon snake (30).

# Gulf Coast Ribbon Snake

*Thamnophis proximus orarius*

☐ *Area of intergradation*

This coastal plain serpent is seen most frequently in open prairie—near the Gulf these reptiles bask on the low dirt levees that impound rice field irrigation lakes—though wooded terrain is also inhabited. Notable for its mint-green cheeks, chartreuse belly, and less contrasting dorsal pattern than its upland counterparts', *T. p. orarius* has a brownish-green back whose pale vertebral line is almost the same color as its olive-tan side stripes. Individuals from eastern Harris County and southern Liberty County may have a golden spinal stripe, however, with a back and sides nearly as dark as those of the western ribbon.

In studying a woodland population of these animals on the Sarpy Wildlife Refuge, a cypress-gum swamp northwest of New Orleans, Donald Tinkle (Ecology 38 [1]:69–77, 1957) established from recapture of marked individuals that they ordinarily occupy loosely defined home territories several acres in size. Though his specimens apparently foraged throughout the study area, Tinkle more often encountered them on earthen ridges extending into the swamp than in any other microenvironment. (In spring, when temperatures were still cool, the ribbon snakes avoided the shady portion of the ridges during periods of inactivity, preferring to bask in the sunny upper layers of matted blackberry vines, while in hot summer weather they sought the protection of the wooded parts of the ridges.) In this subtropical climate these little reptiles are active almost year-round, but *orarius'* most extensive foraging was found to occur immediately after warm summer rains, when its frog and toad prey is most plentiful.

Reproduction is similar to that of the western ribbon snake (30), except that breeding appears to begin somewhat earlier in the season: gravid individuals were discovered as early as April, while by July, 88 percent of females turned out to be pregnant.

Size, scalation, and behavior are similar to that of the western ribbon snake (30).

# Arid Land Ribbon Snake

*Thamnophis proximus diabolicus*

☐ *Area of intergradation*

Ribbon snakes' ability to subsist around even small bodies of water allows this westernmost race of *Thamnophis proximus* to occupy much of West Texas. Keeping to river courses across the High Plains, it occurs as far upstream on the Pecos River as Artesia, New Mexico, and is entirely absent only from the driest parts of the northern Chihuahuan Desert. Moreover, these animals have now moved well beyond the heads of the narrow creeks—to which they were previously restricted on the dry shortgrass prairie—by colonizing the ubiquitous Panhandle stock tanks that provide their frog and toad prey an aquatic reproductive niche from which to snap up the flies drawn to the manure-covered banks.

Because the type specimen was taken near the Devil's River, this snake owes its subspecies name to the Greek *diabolikos*. Its back is usually gray-brown—though individuals from the Canadian and Cimarron river drainages sometimes display a darker ground color—with both a distinctive thin black ventrolateral seam and a broad orange vertebral stripe that lightens to gold on the nape.

Throughout the Panhandle, *T. p. diabolicus*—whose record length is just over 4 feet—intergrades with the western ribbon (30), which generally has a darker back and a slightly narrower vertebral stripe. Likewise, on the Stockton and western Edwards plateaus the arid land ribbon intergrades with the redstripe ribbon (31)—the latter having a ruddier vertebral stripe than the arid land—while as far northwest as Laredo on the Rio Grande plain the arid land race's range overlaps that of the olive-backed, vertebrally greenish-tan-striped Gulf Coast ribbon (32).

Size, scalation, reproduction, and behavior are similar to that of the western ribbon snake (30).

*Area of intergradation*

# Texas Patchnose Snake

*Salvadora grahamiae lineata*

***Nonvenomous***   When first captured, a large patchnose may flail about and even give a single panicky nip, but if handled gently it will become calm within moments and rarely bites again. The upper rear teeth are slightly enlarged, while observations suggest that the patchnose's saliva may be somewhat toxic to small lizards.

***Abundance***   One of the most common terrestrial serpents, occurring in almost every well-vegetated rural habitat throughout its range.

***Size***   Adults generally measure between 20 and 34 inches in length; the record is just under 4 feet.

***Habitat***   Common throughout the woodland and farmland mosaic of the central Cross Timbers—where they are found along the intersection of meadow and oak-elm stands—and the oak-juniper savannah of the Edwards Plateau, Texas patchnoses are much less abundant in the thorn brush country of South Texas. Microhabitat includes shelter beneath flat rocks, fallen branches, logs, or planks and corrugated siding around old farms.

***Prey***   On the basis of the feeding preferences of captives, mainly lizards. Smaller snakes, mice, frogs, and buried reptile eggs rooted out with the aid of the big flat rostral scale at the tip of the snout may be important in the diet as well.

***Reproduction***   Egg-bearing. On April 1—when most serpents in the region have just begun courtship—a Palo Pinto County female laid 10 adhesive-shelled yellowish-white eggs averaging 1⅛ inches in length and ⅝ inch in diameter. Two other clutches, numbering 5 and 7 respectively, were laid by Travis County females during the first week in May. Although patterned like the adults, the hatchlings are slightly paler in color, with almost cream-colored sides that darken with age; the largest *S. g. lineata* have blackish dorsal and olive-brown lateral pigmentation.

***Coloring/scale form***   The dorsal scales are smooth and arranged in 17 rows at midbody; a very thin brown side stripe seams the third row of scales above the belly on the foreparts, the second row on the posterior trunk; the cream-colored ventral scales may bear a faint blue-green cast; and the anal plate is divided.

*PATCHNOSE SNAKES*

**Similar snakes**  Northeastern Terrell County, at about the 2,500-foot elevation level, marks the boundary where the Texas patchnose begins to intergrade with its western subspecies, the **mountain patchnose (35)**. This race has unstriped pastel gray sides and a faintly peach-hued vertebral stripe 3 scale rows in width (the Texas form's spinal stripe occupies only the vertebral scale row plus half of each adjacent row), bordered by a pair of slightly narrower blackish dorsolateral lines. **Garter (23–29)** and **ribbon (30–33) snakes** have darker, often checkered backs, at least 19 midbody rows of keeled dorsal scales, and an undivided anal plate. They lack a large flat rostral scale, and most have a pair of small white dots on the rear of the crown.

**Behavior**  Diurnal, terrestrial, and fast-moving, *S. g. lineata* is usually seen only as a yellow and brown streak disappearing through high grass or into a thicket.

*Area of intergradation*

# Mountain Patchnose Snake

*Salvadora grahamiae grahamiae*

**Nonvenomous**   A docile little serpent that rarely bites even when handled in the field.

**Abundance**   Widely distributed and fairly common in suitable microhabitat throughout its range.

**Size**   Slightly shorter than the Texas patchnose, the mountain race usually measures between 18 and 30 inches in length; the record is 37½ inches.

**Habitat**   *S. g. grahamiae* occurs throughout the Trans-Pecos in a variety of stony and/or brushy situations, especially—in the succulent desert west of the Devil's River—the heart-root cavities under decaying agaves and sotol.

**Prey**   Primarily lizards, although other serpents, reptile eggs, and mice are also eaten.

**Reproduction**   Egg-bearing. See Texas patchnose snake (34).

**Coloring/scale form**   An enlarged rostral overlaps the adjacent nasal scales to the side and folds back over the snout, giving this species its distinctive squared-off profile as well as its common name. The 17 midbody rows of dorsal scales are smooth, there are usually 8 upper labials, the posterior chin shields beneath its lower jaw either touch or are separated by a single small scale, and the anal plate is divided.

**Similar snakes**   The subspecies **Texas patchnose (34)** has a narrower pale orange vertebral line bordered by a pair of wider blackish-brown dorsolateral stripes; its buff lower sides are split by a thin dark seam along the third scale row above its belly. The **Big Bend patchnose (36)** is distinguished by the line of tiny dark hash marks along the fourth lateral scale row above its peach-colored belly, its 9 upper labial scales, and the 2 or 3 small scales that separate its posterior underchin shields. **Garter (23–29)** and **ribbon (30–33) snakes** are predominantly dark-backed animals with a narrower pale vertebral stripe, at least 19 rows of keeled dorsal scales, and an undivided anal plate. Unlike the patchnose, garters and ribbons have no enlarged rostral scale.

**Behavior**   Quick and elusive in brush or near cover, the patchnose must still rely on ambush to obtain most of its even faster-moving prey, typically employing a series of short glides interspersed with long periods of waiting. Once in range, it may seize a lizard up to twice its own diameter, hanging on doggedly as its victim drags it back and forth. Though it may take half an hour, the patchnose will steadily work its way forward along the tiring lacertilian's body to the snout, then, stretching its delicate head and jaws over the larger skull of the lizard, eventually squeeze the animal into its throat.

*PATCHNOSE SNAKES*

# Big Bend Patchnose Snake

*Salvadora deserticola*

**Nonvenomous**   A calm reptile that generally does not bite, even when first handled in the field.

**Abundance**   This predominantly Mexican species is uncommon within its restricted Texas range.

**Size**   Twenty to 45 inches in length. Even the largest individuals are quite delicate in configuration.

**Habitat**   Shrub desert, tobosa-grama grassland, and catclaw-creosote-blackbrush flats, as well as broken upland terrain.

**Prey**   Lizards, snakes, reptile eggs, and small rodents; all but the latter are sometimes rooted out of sand-filled depressions with the aid of the enlarged rostral scale.

**Reproduction**   Egg-bearing. See Texas patchnose snake (34).

**Coloring/scale form**   An exceptionally attractive serpent whose yellowish-gray sides are separated from its wide peach dorsal stripe by a flanking pair of dark brown dorsolateral lines. The enlarged rostral scale, widest immediately above the mouth (where it overlaps the adjacent nasal scales), covers the tip of the snout in a distinctive flat patch from which the common name is derived. Below, the lips and throat are unmarked white––either 2 or 3 small scales separate the posterior underchin shields—while the belly is pale peach. There are 9 upper labial scales, the smooth dorsal scales are arranged in 17 rows at midbody, and the anal plate is divided.

*Underchin: Texas and mountain patchnose snakes*     *Underchin: Big Bend patchnose snake*

**Similar snakes**   The **mountain patchnose (35)** has unstriped sides, 8 upper labials, a cream-colored belly, and posterior underchin shields that either touch or are separated by a single scale. **Garter (23–29)** and **ribbon (30–33) snakes** have dark backs, a narrower, light yellow to orangish vertebral stripe, at least 19 rows of keeled dorsal scales, and an undivided anal plate; they lack the patchnose's enlarged rostral.

**Behavior**   Like many diurnal desert serpents, the Big Bend patchnose is inclined to midday basking in cool weather, adopting a predominantly crepuscular activity pattern during the heat of July, August, and September.

# Rough Green Snake

*Opheodrys aestivus*

***Nonvenomous***   Green snakes do not bite humans.

***Abundance***   Widespread and, in suitable habitat throughout the eastern two thirds of the state, abundant.

***Size***   Adults are most often between 22 and 32 inches in length; the record is 45⅝ inches.

***Habitat***   Primarily arboreal, the rough green prefers leafy trees and shrubs with closely spaced stems that allow it to move about readily; this niche is found most often along the sunlit edges of both pine and deciduous woods bordering streams and ponds, roadways, and other open areas.

***Prey***   Plucked daintily from leaves and stems, most of the rough green's food animals are caterpillars, spiders, grasshoppers, crickets, and, near water, dragonflies and mayflies.

***Reproduction***   Egg-bearing. Three to 12 proportionately large eggs are laid beneath leaf litter. The young are greenish gray and at hatching measure from 6 to 8⅝ inches in length; they reach adult size after about a year but do not breed until their second spring.

***Coloring/scale form***   Despite being commonly called grass snake, this slender, emerald-backed reptile is color-adapted instead to the verdant hue of tree leaves (except on lawns, grass is seldom as vividly green). The lips, chin, and belly are yellow. Arranged in 17 rows at midbody, the dorsal scales are keeled; the anal plate is divided.

***Similar snakes***   Both predominantly terrestrial and extremely rare in Texas, the **western smooth green snake (38)** is a slightly smaller species with 15 rows of smooth dorsal scales that occurs in only a few counties along the upper Gulf Coast. Adult **eastern yellowbelly (64)** and **Mexican (65) racers** are more robust, olive-brown-backed serpents with smooth scales. Each of their nostrils is centered in a single nasal plate, while both green snake species have nostrils that lie across the juncture of adjacent nasal scales. **Schott's (62)** and **Ruthven's (63) whipsnakes** have thin white lateral lines and smooth dorsal scales arranged in 15 rows at midbody.

***Behavior***   Slow-moving, unwary, and easy to capture, *O. aestivus* depends almost exclusively on camouflage for protection: when approached, it often responds by freezing, sometimes swaying slightly with the wind to match the movement of surrounding foliage.

*GREEN SNAKES*

# Western Smooth Green Snake

*Opheodrys vernalis blanchardi*

**Nonvenomous**   Its quiet disposition and small size ensure that this little reptile is completely harmless to humans.

**Abundance**   In Texas *O. v. blanchardi* is known from fewer than 10 specimens, all collected on the coastal plain of Austin, Chambers, Harris, and Matagorda counties.

**Size**   The longest of the Texas specimens was just over 15 inches, the smallest a bit more than 10 inches.

**Habitat**   The few remaining mesic prairie communities still covered with native short grasses.

**Prey**   Prey is probably similar to that of the rough green snake: mainly insects (especially crickets, caterpillars, and grasshoppers), as well as spiders and snails.

**Reproduction**   Egg-bearing, with occasional reports of communal nesting sites. The young have an olive- to light brown dorsal hue that persists into adulthood on many specimens whose littermates may have acquired emerald backs within a few weeks of hatching.

**Coloring/scale form**   Usually bright green above (see Reproduction), with a white or pale yellow belly. The dorsal scales are smooth and arranged in 15 rows at midbody; the anal plate is divided.

**Similar snakes**   The far more common **rough green snake (37)** is similar in color but is both longer and a bit more slimly proportioned, with 17 rows of keeled dorsal scales. **Eastern yellowbelly racers (64)** also have 17 midbody rows of dorsal scales, as well as brown-blotched backs as juveniles—the only time they are as small as the patternless western smooth green. Racers' nasal openings are centered in a single plate, while green snakes' nostrils lie across the juncture of adjacent nasal scales.

**Behavior**   *O. vernalis* (the Latin name means "spring snake") is active during daylight, foraging through dense grass and, unlike the predominantly arboreal rough green, seldom climbing even into low bushes. Most Texas specimens have been found only after the high water of a severe storm or hurricane covered wide areas of low-lying coastal plain.

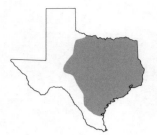

# Texas
# Rat Snake
*Elaphe obsoleta lindheimeri*

**Nonvenomous**  Texas rat snakes are among the most aggressive non-venomous serpents in the state: if threatened, most bite readily, though the pressure of their jaws is so light that only pricks and shallow scratches result.

**Abundance**  The most common long, dark, brown-mottled snake occurring in suburban areas throughout the eastern half of Texas—and the only one likely to be found high in trees or hidden in barn rafters, attics, or abandoned automobiles and machinery. Immediately after they hatch in late summer and early autumn, the brown-blotched, grayish young are among the most frequently encountered small terrestrial serpents—as well as perhaps the hottest-tempered, typically nipping without hesitation when picked up.

**Size**  *E. o. lindheimeri* is recorded to just over 7 feet in length, although the slim, wiry-trunked adults average 42 to 72 inches.

**Habitat**  Abundant in both deciduous woods and pastureland, this reptile also occurs in a variety of other environments, from East Texas pine forest to swampy coastal prairie.

**Prey**  Prey is primarily warm-blooded: birds and their nestlings, rodents, and other small mammals; animals too vigorous to be swallowed without resistance are first squeezed in a loop of the well-muscled trunk.

**Reproduction**  Egg-bearing. Like those of other rat snakes, the 1¾-by-1-inch smooth-shelled eggs are covered with a sticky substance that may cause the entire clutch to adhere in a single cluster. The 12- to 14½-inch-long hatchlings have lead-gray crowns striped with a pair of solid chocolate-colored lines that join to form a forward-facing, spearpoint-shaped marking; across the eyes another chocolate band extends no farther rearward than the posterior upper labial scales.

**Coloring/scale form**  Reddish skin is often evident between the scales covering the sides of the neck, while the predominantly pale belly is generally blotched with dark squares partially obscured by a grayish overwash. The underside of the tail tip is usually solid gray. Of the 27 midbody rows of dorsal scales, only those along the spine are strongly keeled; the anal plate is divided.

*LARGE, BROWN-BLOTCHED TERRESTRIAL SNAKES*

***Similar snakes*** Adult **Baird's rat snakes (40)** lack cross-dorsal blotches and are usually faintly marked with 4 dark longitudinal stripes. Juvenile **Great Plains rat snakes (41)** closely resemble young *lindheimeri* except for the pair of black-edged brown lines that describe a V on their whitish crowns; a similarly black-edged brown stripe runs across the snout, masks the eyes, and continues past the upper labial scales onto the neck. The brown dorsal scales are separated by no more than 3 rows of paler scales (*lindheimeri* has 4 or more), and the underside of its tail is striped with white all the way to the tip. The brown dorsal blotches of the nonarboreal **prairie kingsnake (43)** are also usually edged with black, its vertebral scales are smooth, and its anal plate is undivided. The **bullsnake (50)** has a speckled crown much lighter than its neck, a chocolate-banded yellowish tail, 4 prefrontal scales (rat snakes have the conventional pair of prefrontals), at least 29 rows of dorsal scales, and an undivided anal plate.

***Behavior*** With its wiry, slightly laterally flattened body and sharp-edged belly scales that can dig like spikes into tree bark, the Texas rat snake is an agile climber; it also swims well and is sometimes found patrolling creek banks from the water.

# Baird's Rat Snake

### *Elaphe bairdi*

**Nonvenomous**  Although some individuals are among the least aggressive of large snakes, other Baird's rat snakes may hiss and nip if cornered.

**Abundance**  Spottily dispersed throughout both the central hill country and the Trans-Pecos, but nowhere abundant.

**Size**  Most adults are between 24 and 40 inches long; one enormous specimen measured 62 inches.

**Habitat**  Principally the Cretaceous limestone canyons of the Edwards Plateau, as well as both upland and desert parts of the Trans-Pecos.

**Prey**  Like most rat snakes, the Baird's is a generalized predator, constricting a variety of prey that includes birds and their eggs, lizards, rodents, and other small mammals.

**Reproduction**  Egg-bearing. Mating during May and early June results in the deposition of usually fewer than 10 leathery, adhesive-shelled eggs in midsummer. These hatch in about 3 months into 11- to 13-inch-long transversely brown-lined gray offspring. (During their second year the prominent cross-dorsal pattern of young *bairdi* gradually merges into the faint longitudinal stripes of the adult.)

**Coloring/scale form**  Beneath a translucent sheen, the forebody is washed with a golden tint—the result of myriad tiny orangish crescents, one of which rims the forward margin of each anterior dorsal scale. (A rare, yellowish-tan color phase dimly marked with gray longitudinal stripes occurs just west of Big Bend.) Lips and chin are light gray-brown to pale yellow, which continues beneath the fore- and midbody, then darkens to pale salmon, scalloped with gray, under the tail. The faintly keeled dorsal scales are arranged in 27 rows at midbody, and the anal plate is divided.

**Similar snakes**  The adult **Texas rat snake (39)** has a dark brown head and neck, as well as rectangular chocolate blotches along its otherwise light brown trunk. The mustard-tan color of the **Trans-Pecos rat snake (42)** is distinctive, as are its black, roughly H-shaped dorsal pattern and the ring of small scales that borders the lower margin of its eye.

**Behavior**  Baird's rat snakes are for the most part calm, slow-moving serpents whose temperament is generally unlike that of their very close relative, the aggressive Texas rat snake.

*LARGE, BROWN-BLOTCHED TERRESTRIAL SNAKES*

# Great Plains Rat Snake

*Elaphe guttata emoryi*

**Nonvenomous**  Although large individuals may nip if picked up roughly, most are docile and easily handled.

**Abundance**  Abundant and widely distributed, *E. g. emoryi* may be found in nearly every terrestrial macrohabitat within the state; it is most numerous on the southern coastal plain, however.

**Size**  Adults usually measure between 2½ and 3½ feet in length; the record is 60¼ inches.

**Habitat**  Varies from open grassland—this snake is quite common on the prairie near Corpus Christi—to mountainous or swampy woodland, desert, and South Texas thorn brush.

**Prey**  Warm-blooded animals, killed by constriction: especially rodents, as well as ground-nesting birds and their young, frogs, and lizards. Smaller snakes are not ordinarily taken as prey.

**Reproduction**  Egg-bearing. The 5 to 25 young range in length from 11 to 15 inches at hatching, and may grow to 29 inches after 14 months.

**Coloring/scale form**  The Great Plains rat snake's most distinctive physical attribute is the diamond-shaped marking described by 2 brown stripes that join on its pale gray crown in a point whose apex lies between the eyes. On the underside of the tail, the squarish, gray-brown ventral blotches coalesce into a pair of dark distal stripes, between which a pale central line continues all the way to the tip. The dorsal scales, arranged in 27 to 29 midbody rows, are weakly keeled along the spine, smooth elsewhere; the anal plate is divided.

**Similar snakes**  The very similar-looking **prairie kingsnake (43)** is more brownish or olive (rather than gray) above, with an obscure dark marking on its crown that usually points rearward; its dorsal scales are smooth, its anal plate is undivided. **Bullsnakes (50)** have heavily keeled dorsal scales and speckled crowns paler than their necks. There are 4 prefrontal scales (2 in rat snakes) and an undivided anal plate. Adult **Texas rat snakes (39)** have solid dark brown heads and necks and uniformly gray undertails. Juveniles are distinguished by the lead-gray rather than whitish ground color of their crowns and the solid chocolate eye mask that runs no farther rearward than the corner of the jaw. **Glossy snakes (53–55)** have a pale little vertebral line along the nape of the neck, an unmarked white belly, and an undivided anal plate.

**Behavior**  Extremely nocturnal throughout its March-to-late-October activity period, *E. g. emoryi* ordinarily emerges only well after dark from under the rocks and logs where it spends the daylight hours.

# Trans-Pecos
# Rat Snake
*Elaphe subocularis*

**Nonvenomous**  Trans-Pecos rat snakes almost never defend themselves against human beings.

**Abundance**  Widespread and sometimes locally common, though seen only at night and in warm weather, mostly on little-traveled back roads in Val Verde, Terrell, and southwestern Brewster counties during the breeding season in late May and June.

**Size**  A majority of adults measure between 30 and 48 inches in length, but individuals have been recorded to 5½ feet.

**Habitat**  Predominantly rocky terrain in the northern Chihuahuan Desert, generally below 5,000 feet in elevation, including barren flats and succulent-desert slopes of ocotillo, lechuguilla, and sotol cactus. A less severe environment in which this species also occurs is the oak-juniper woodland of West Texas' mountain islands.

**Prey**  A generalized feeder on almost any smaller vertebrate, with the probable exception of other snakes.

**Reproduction**  Egg-bearing. First accomplished at the Dallas Zoo during the 1960's, captive breeding has since become widespread. Delicate little creatures averaging 11½ to 13 inches in length at hatching, the young are paler than the adults but share the same dorsal pattern.

**Coloring/scale form**  *E. subocularis* is unique among North American serpents in possessing 40 pairs of chromosomes instead of the typical allotment of 36 or 38. Scalation is also unusual for a rat snake, with a row of small subocular scales separating the upper lip scales from the big dark eyes that are responsible for its appealing demeanor. On more distinctly marked individuals, 2 parallel blackish dorsolateral lines are joined across the spine in an H-shaped pattern by 27 to 41 crossbars that become small saddles on the tail. *Subocularis* from the lower Pecos River drainage are lighter and grayer and lack much of the dark vertebral patterning, while among the rare yellowish-cream Trans-Pecos rat snakes of southwestern Brewster County, the faint, rounded dorsal blotches are entirely separate; gray-ground-colored *E. subocularis* inhabit the Franklin Mountains of El Paso. The belly is off-white under the throat and chin, darkening to pale olive-buff by midbody; some individuals show very dim undertail striping. Only the 7 central rows of dorsal scales, which occur in 31 to 35 rows at midbody, are keeled. The anal plate is divided.

*LARGE, BROWN-BLOTCHED TERRESTRIAL SNAKES*

**Similar snakes**  None; no other Texas serpent shares either this animal's unique dorsolateral coloration or its distinctive vertebral pattern.

**Behavior**  Like other desert-living reptiles, *Elaphe subocularis* responds to the harsh climate of its northern Chihuahuan Desert range by restricting its movements on the surface to dry, temperate summer nights. During the day, as well as during brumation, it withdraws into mammal burrows or descends to subterranean niches through the labyrinth of broken limestone that underlies much of the desert floor.

# Prairie Kingsnake

*Lampropeltis calligaster calligaster*

***Nonvenomous***   This generally mild-tempered reptile may vibrate its tail in fear, but it seldom nips humans, even when handled.

***Abundance***   Widely distributed but uncommon throughout the eastern half of the state.

***Size***   Adults average 2 to 3 feet in length; the record is 58⅛ inches.

***Habitat***   Mostly open grassland: the tallgrass prairie of Central and North Central Texas; moist salt-grass savannah along the upper Gulf Coast; piles of driftwood on the landward side of barrier beaches from Lavaca Bay to Sabine Pass; less frequently, rocky hillside pasture and riparian woodland.

***Prey***   This powerful constrictor is more oriented toward warm-blooded prey than other kingsnakes: recorded food animals include mice, rats, gophers, moles, and birds, as well as frogs and toads, lizards, and other snakes.

***Reproduction***   Egg-bearing. In earthen cavities several inches below the surface, clutches of 6 to 17 smooth-shelled eggs are deposited during late June and July. Though wild individuals are unlikely to live as long, one specimen has been maintained at the Oklahoma City Zoo for over 13 years.

***Coloring/scale form***   Prairie kingsnakes occur in a wide range of color variations, some of which are very dark, with dorsal blotches that run together to form an almost solid umber hue or even combine to form 4 faint dusky stripes. (*Calligaster* means "beautiful belly," a reference to the large, squarish brown splotches spaced along the whitish, faintly gray-mottled underparts.) The smooth dorsal scales are arranged in 25 to 27 midbody rows and the anal plate is undivided.

***Similar snakes***   Very similar in appearance, the **Great Plains rat snake (41)** has weakly keeled vertebral scales, while its ground color is more gray than olive-brown, with a dark-edged, spearpoint-shaped marking that points forward on the pale crown; the undertail tip has a pale central stripe (the king's is unmarked) and a divided anal plate. The **bullsnake (50)** has large square blotches on its back; its yellowish tail is crossbanded with dark brown, and its freckled head is much lighter in color than its neck. There are 4 preocular scales (kingsnakes have but the conventional 2) as well as 29 or more rows of keeled dorsal scales. **Texas (53)** and **Kansas (54) glossy snakes** have a pale longitudinal line along the nape, at least 29 rows of dorsal scales, and an unmarked white belly.

***Behavior***   Prairie kings are secretive animals that seldom emerge from beneath rocks, clumps of grass, or the depths of small-mammal burrows except for foraging, which takes place mostly at night during the hottest months, at dusk in spring and fall.

*LARGE, BROWN-BLOTCHED TERRESTRIAL SNAKES*

# Eastern Hognose Snake

*Heterodon platyrhinos*

**Nonvenomous**  The eastern hognose is one of the few sizable snakes that never bite humans. Its enlarged rear teeth—designed to introduce its very mild salivary toxins into small amphibian prey—are located too far back in its throat to be used against a larger adversary.

**Abundance**  Common in most of its range.

**Size**  Adults ordinarily measure between 20 and 33 inches in length; the record is 45½ inches.

**Habitat**  Open deciduous or pine woods and forest-grassland near streams, ponds, or lakes seem to be the most frequented habitats.

**Prey**  Although toads generally make up the greatest part of the diet, frogs, where abundant, may also be a principal food. There are reports of small carrion scavenging, while hatchlings will take crickets.

**Reproduction**  Egg-bearing. Mating occurs from March through early May, followed some 6 weeks later by deposition of the 4 to 61 (average 22) 1¼-by-¾-inch whitish eggs; the hatchlings measure between 6½ and 9½ inches in length.

**Coloring/scale form**  Since *H. platyrhinos*' back and sides can be nearly any color—from black to reddish- or olive-blotched brown—the hognose is best identified by its stocky trunk, its short head scarcely distinct from its wide neck, and its pointed, upturned snout flanked by sharp-edged little ridges that line the sides of its upper lip. A slight bulge over the eyes is emphasized by the forwardmost of the 2 brown bands that cross the crown on lighter-hued individuals, while a rearward extension of this stripe continues through the dark little eye to the corner of the mouth; a long blackish blotch occupies each side of the neck. The underside of the tail is lighter in hue than the unpatterned grayish belly. Arranged in 23 to 25 rows at midbody, the dorsal scales are heavily keeled; the anal plate is divided.

**Similar snakes**  The **dusty (45)**, **Mexican (47)**, and **plains (46) western hognose** subspecies have a sandy ground color uniformly patterned with big brown dorsolateral spots; their bellies and undertails are heavily blotched with black. **Southern (98)** and **broad-banded (99) copperheads'** reddish-brown bands completely cross the back and sides, and the slender neck is much narrower than the flat-sided head characterized by a dark pit between the nostril and the big pale, vertically slit-pupilled eye.

**Behavior**   Uniquely adapted for burrowing, the eastern hognose is covered with rough-keeled, high-traction scales that enable it to use both its muscular trunk and its wedgelike snout to plow its way through the earth, forcing loosened soil to the sides. In the open its deliberate pace makes it an easy target for predators, though, in defense against whom it has only an elaborate pattern of behavior evolved to make it as unappealing as possible to carnivores. If molested, it may coil or raise its head, flatten its forebody by spreading the long foreribs (from which the common name "spreading adder" is derived), and make feinting pseudo-strikes, often by jerking the head *backward*, yet somehow suggesting the aggressive style of the vipers. Emitting a sharp hiss with each breath, the hognose may then conceal its head under its tightly spiraled tail, writhe convulsively, regurgitate, and discharge a foul-smelling musk from its anal glands. Finally, it may turn belly-up with its tongue hanging loosely from its open jaw—to all appearances a moribund carcass. If placed right side up it will even flop back over, righting itself to crawl away only after the danger has passed.

# Dusty Hognose Snake

*Heterodon nasicus gloydi*

**Mildly venomous** *Heterodon* means "different-" or "multiple-toothed," in reference to this genus' combination of conventional anterior teeth and large hinged rear ones. Although mildly toxic to its amphibian and lizard prey, the western hognose's saliva is not dangerous to humans, while the tips of its long rear teeth lie so far back in the throat that they can be used only for channeling the seromucous parotid gland secretions into partially swallowed food animals too vigorous to be engulfed further. This opalescent saliva could probably cause a mild inflammatory reaction in human beings, but the dusty hognose is so docile that no amount of provocation will cause it even to open its mouth in defense against a human assailant.

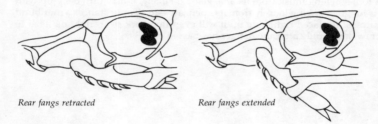

*Rear fangs retracted*          *Rear fangs extended*

**Abundance**  Rather uncommon, occurring in widely separated populations over much of its Texas range.

**Size**  Adult *H. n. gloydi* are typically 17 to 25 inches long; the record is nearly 3 feet.

**Habitat**  Sandy shortgrass prairie; rocky semidesert; pasture and woodland interface. On the upper coastal islands dusty hognoses occur both on salt-grass prairie and in residential neighborhoods.

**Prey**  Amphibians, lizards, smaller snakes, and reptile eggs, as well as new-born rodents and the young of ground-nesting birds.

**Reproduction**  Egg-bearing. Some evidence indicates that breeding occurs only in alternate years. Laid between early June and August, the 4 to 23 eggs hatch after 52 to 64 days into young between 6 and 7½ inches long; they reach adult size and sexual maturity at 18 to 24 months of age.

**Coloring/scale form**   In 1952, R. A. Edgren divided the western hognose population into the 3 subspecies recognized today: dusty, plains, and Mexican. The dusty race is characterized by the fewer than 32 medium-sized brown dorsal blotches between snout and vent in males, fewer than 37 in females (males can be identified by their slightly thicker-based tails). *H. n. gloydi* also has 9 to 28 small azygous scales separating the prefrontal plates of its forecrown. The plains hognose (46) is characterized by more than 35 slightly smaller dorsal blotches over the same area in males, more than 40 in females, and the same number of azygous cephalic scales as the dusty. The Mexican hognose (47) is marked like the dusty, but with no more than 6 little azygous scales between its prefrontal plates. In all 3 subspecies, the sandy-buff back is thoroughly blotched with big oval dorsolateral spots, while smaller brown patches occur on the lower sides, above the predominantly black belly, which is scattered with white or yellowish blotches. Arranged in 23 rows at midbody, the dorsal scales are heavily keeled; the anal plate is divided.

**Similar snakes**   The only serpent living within *H. n. gloydi*'s range that closely resembles it is the **eastern hognose (44),** which may be either uniformly dark above or patterned with pale, rectangular vertebral blotches (between blackish blotches) on a variable but generally darker brown ground color. Its undertail is much lighter in hue than its belly. **Western (48) hooknose snakes** are rarely as much as a foot in length and have minuscule upturned snouts without a perpendicular reinforcing keel, irregular dark dorsolateral crossbands, and 17 midbody rows of smooth dorsal scales.

**Behavior**   *H. n. gloydi*'s behavioral imperative against biting a large adversary is so strong that it will gag on a finger poked into its open mouth rather than close its jaws.

# Plains Hognose Snake

*Heterodon nasicus nasicus*

**Mildly venomous**   *H. n. nasicus* does not bite humans, but it often strikes vigorously (though with the mouth clamped firmly shut so that an assailant is only bumped by the snout) before resorting to a mild version of the characteristic hognose tactic of feigning death. See eastern hognose snake (44), Behavior.

**Abundance**   This race is uncommon throughout most of its Panhandle range.

**Size**   Adults are generally 15 to 25 inches long; the largest Texas specimen, a male from Hale County, measured 35¼ inches.

**Habitat**   Preferred macrohabitat is the short- and mixed-grass prairie of the High Plains, mainly where canyons or large draws provide at least seasonal water, where there is a gravelly or sandy soil that ensures easy burrowing, and where leaf litter or other ground cover is available.

**Prey**   See dusty hognose snake (45).

**Reproduction**   Similar to that of the dusty hognose (45). Because these reptiles winter in scattered solitary dens, during the first weeks after springtime emergence the males wander widely in search of mates; a brief period of copulation also occurs in the fall, with spermatozoa from the autumn pairings remaining viable in the cloaca throughout the winter. Since many females examined in midsummer are not gravid, however, much of the population may breed only in alternate years.

**Coloring/scale form**   Large parts of the mostly coal-black belly pigment are edged with white, yellow, or pale orange; see dusty hognose snake (45).

**Similar snakes**   The **eastern hognose (44)** has a marginally less upturned snout, the underside of its tail is lighter in hue than its unmarked gray belly, and its dorsal pattern never involves a pale tan ground color broken only by small brown vertebral and lateral splotches. **Western hooknose snakes (48)** are much smaller, crossbanded reptiles distinguished by their 17 rows of smooth dorsal scales and, in place of the hognoses' raised postrostral keel, a shallow depression behind their tiny hooked snouts.

**Behavior**   Field studies of *H. n. nasicus* in central Kansas show it to be active mostly morning and evening, sheltering at night and during cold weather by burrowing into sandy soil. It seems to be less dependent on hiding beneath flat objects lying on the surface than most terrestrial serpents, although it may be found in leaf litter.

# Mexican Hognose Snake

*Heterodon nasicus kennerlyi*

**Mildly venomous**   See dusty hognose snake (45).

**Abundance**   The Mexican hognose is uncommon in the Trans-Pecos but moderately abundant in the thorn brush country of the lower Rio Grande plain.

**Size**   Similar to that of the plains hognose (46), usually 15 to 25 inches long.

**Habitat**   Two considerably different habitats prevail. In South Texas Mexican hognoses occur in thorn woodland, most often near arroyos or watercourses, while in the Trans-Pecos *H. n. kennerlyi* is largely a prairie-living animal.

**Prey**   Similar to that of the dusty hognose (45); carrion is also occasionally eaten.

**Reproduction**   See dusty hognose snake (45).

**Coloring/scale form**   See dusty hognose snake (45).

**Similar snakes**   See dusty hognose snake (45). Exhibiting almost the same dorsal coloring, size, and body configuration as the Mexican hognose is the **desert massasauga (109),** which shares both of the hognose's ranges; except by looking for the viper's rattle, it is often difficult to tell at a glance which animal is at hand. The **Mexican hooknose snake (49)** is a smaller, less prominently marked serpent with 17 rows of dorsal scales (the hognose has 23) and a shallow depression rather than a raised keel behind its tiny upturned snout.

**Behavior**   In South Texas, *kennerlyi*'s activity generally follows a seasonal pattern, with most appearances being recorded in May, June, and September, when over the course of a few days several individuals may turn up in places where no others have been seen for months.

*LARGE, BROWN-BLOTCHED TERRESTRIAL SNAKES*

# Western Hooknose Snake

*Gyalopion canum*

**Nonvenomous**   These gentle little serpents never bite humans.

**Abundance**   For nearly a century this species was thought to be extremely rare; now, due to increased reporting of observations, *Gyalopion canum* is known to be not uncommon over much of the northeastern Trans-Pecos and the northern Stockton Plateau.

**Size**   Most western hooknoses are between 6½ and 11 inches in length; the record is 14¼ inches.

**Habitat**   Principally shortgrass prairie above 2,500 feet in elevation; much less often, both the oak-juniper savannah of the western Edwards Plateau and the northwest-central plains.

**Prey**   Spiders, centipedes, and scorpions that share its semisubterranean microhabitat.

**Reproduction**   Egg-bearing. All that is known about this species' reproduction is that in early July one captive female laid a single, proportionately large, 1⅛-inch-long egg.

**Coloring/scale form**   The most distinctive characteristic of this stub-tailed little reptile is the upturned hook on the tip of its snout. The faintly speckled buff dorsolateral ground color is crossed with brown transverse bars with zigzag black-lined edges, which taper to points just above the off-white belly. Except for being pocked with tiny apical pits, the dorsal scales are smooth and arranged in 17 rows at midbody; the rostral scale splits the internasals but reaches back only as far as the juncture of the prefrontal scales; and the anal plate is divided.

**Similar snakes**   The **Mexican hooknose snake (49)** has an either unpatterned or less strongly banded crown, as well as narrower, often poorly defined dorsolateral crossbands. There are usually no internasal scales; the large rostral extends rearward between the prefrontal scales all the way to the frontal plate. The sympatrically ranging **dusty (45)** and **Mexican (47) hognose snakes** are more robust reptiles with 23 rows of keeled dorsal scales, bigger upturned snouts characterized by a longitudinal reinforcing keel, and heavy facial scalation that forms a slight bulge over the eyes.

**Behavior**   Found at the surface mainly under rocks, this slow-gaited little burrower emerges only after dark or, following spring or early summer rains, at dusk. Besides hiding, *G. canum*'s primary protective stratagem is a series of sudden gyrations, apparently useful in discomfiting some predators, that includes extending and retracting the cloaca with a popping sound.

# Mexican Hooknose Snake

*Ficimia streckeri*

**Nonvenomous**  This small animal does not bite human beings.

**Abundance**  Particularly during May and June, *Ficimia streckeri* is fairly common at night on the back roads of Webb, Brooks, Jim Hogg, Duval, Zapata, and Starr counties.

**Size**  Almost all South Texas hooknoses are between 5½ and 9 inches in length; the record is 19 inches.

**Habitat**  Widely distributed throughout the thorn brush woodland of the Rio Grande plain, especially in the vicinity of such man-made sources of water as stock ponds and irrigation canals.

**Prey**  Spiders are the preferred prey, but centipedes and other small invertebrates may also be taken.

**Reproduction**  Egg-bearing.

**Coloring/scale form**  The upturned scale at the tip of the snout has a sharp little point, and except for a large brown spot below the eye, the lips, throat, and lower sides are buff; the belly is off-white. Arranged in 17 rows at midbody, the dorsal scales are smooth, though pocked with tiny apical pits. There are usually no internasal scales; the enlarged rostral occupies this area, separates the prefrontals, and reaches all the way to the frontal scale. The anal plate is divided.

**Similar snakes**  The **western hooknose snake (48)** has internasal scales, a rostral that does not extend as far back as the frontal plate, wider, black-edged brown dorsal crossbands, and a prominently crossbarred crown generally followed by a longitudinal brown blotch along the nape. The larger **Mexican hognose snake (47)** has 23 rows of keeled dorsal scales and a more prominent upturned rostral scale backed by a perpendicular ridge.

**Behavior**  Hooknoses are slow-moving creatures whose principal means of self-defense is an exceptional burrowing ability—when picked up, these little animals vigorously nose downward through their captor's fingers—that allows them to disappear into soft earth within moments. *Ficimia streckeri*'s other defensive tactics include slowly weaving the elevated head and forebody in an approximation of the defensive posture of the vipers, while a threatened individual may also suddenly flip itself back and forth, extending and contracting its cloaca through its vent to produce a popping sound.

*LARGE, BROWN-BLOTCHED TERRESTRIAL SNAKES*

# Bullsnake
*Pituophis melanoleucus sayi*

**Nonvenomous**   Bullsnakes vary greatly in temperament: some wild adults allowthemselves to be picked up without exhibiting any defensive behavior, while even after years in captivity others still rear the head and forebody into an elevated S-shaped curve, hiss menacingly, and attempt to bite almost every time they are handled; none will strike unless molested, however.

**Abundance**   Very common.

**Size**   Most adult bullsnakes range from 3 to 5 feet in length; the largest specimen taken in Texas is the 8-foot-6½-inch Wichita County giant captured by Dr. Robert Kuntz of the San Antonio Herpetological Society.

**Habitat**   One of the most widely distributed serpents in the state, *P. m. sayi* occupies a wide variety of mostly open terrain ranging in elevation from sea level to at least 7,000 feet in the Guadalupe Mountains.

**Prey**   Because of their large size, bullsnakes eat a lot, and as a result are economically beneficial serpents, destroying enough mice, cotton rats, and gophers to mitigate the need for local rodent poisoning. Other prey is also usually warm-blooded: ground squirrels, young rabbits, and sometimes ground-nesting birds; juveniles are reported to eat insects and lizards as well.

**Reproduction**   Egg-bearing. Courtship initially involves springtime olfactory tracking along a pheromonal scent trace laid down by the female. Between 5 and 19 leathery, sticky-shelled eggs from 2 to more than 3½ inches in length are laid in loose soil during June and July; the 12½- to 19-inch-long hatchlings are abundant throughout West and Central Texas after they emerge in early autumn.

**Coloring/scale form**   Of native serpents, only *Pituophis* have khaki-colored, brown-freckled crowns distinctly paler than their light-and-dark block-patterned backs. Often, a slightly elevated transverse ridge—from which the common name is derived—crosses the forehead like the boss of a bovine horn; along it there is usually a slightly darker band that angles back through the eye and across the cheek. Cephalic scalation is also unique: 4 small prefrontal scales back the narrow rostral plate, which is raised above the adjacent scales. Arranged in 29 to 37 rows (usually 33 at midbody), the dorsal scales have apical pits and are most strongly keeled along the spine. The laterally speckled belly is off-white, its anal plate undivided.

***Similar snakes*** The **Louisiana pine snake (51)** is a darker and less distinctly patterned East Texas subspecies distinguished by its fewer than 40 nonrectangular vertebral blotches. The **Sonoran gopher snake (52)** is typically a paler, sometimes reddish-blotched, mostly desert-living subspecies whose rostral scale is broader and lower than that of the bullsnake; in pure form it is found in Texas only in El Paso and Hudspeth counties. Adult **Texas rat snakes (39)** have dark brown heads, 27 rows of dorsal scales, 2 prefrontal scales, and a divided anal plate. **Great Plains rat snakes (41)** also have 2 prefrontals, a divided anal plate, and a dark-edged brown spearpoint marking on the grayish crown. **Texas (53)** and **Kansas (54) glossy snakes** have a pale longitudinal line along the nape, an unmarked white belly, 2 prefrontal scales, and a blotched or spotted rather than crossbanded tail. **Prairie kingsnakes (43)** have no more than 27 rows of smooth dorsal scales and the conventional 2 prefrontals.

***Behavior*** *P. m. sayi* is a relatively slow-moving daylight forager and is therefore particularly vulnerable to human activity; many are run over by cars. Ordinarily entirely terrestrial, bullsnakes can climb fairly well and may scale trees when pursued if no hiding place is available on the ground.

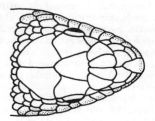

*Prefrontal scales: bull, pine, and gopher snakes*

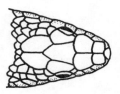

*Prefrontal scales: glossy snakes*

# Louisiana Pine Snake

*Pituophis melanoleucus ruthveni*

***Nonvenomous***   See bullsnake (50).

***Abundance***   Rare, although herpetologists working in Texas' eastern forests have recently turned up a number of individuals, and many more occur in Louisiana. In 1977 this subspecies was protected from capture by the Texas Department of Parks and Wildlife, however.

***Size***   Similar to the bullsnake, although the record is just under 6 feet.

***Habitat***   In spite of its name, the Louisiana pine is not a tree snake but a terrestrial resident of the East Texas and Louisiana hardwood-conifer community, which comprises its only habitat.

***Prey***   Most published records of *P. m. ruthveni* have been of road-killed animals struck during rainy weather at dawn or dusk, indicating probable adherence to the crepuscular foraging pattern typical of serpents that prey on the small mammals most active at these times. The stomachs of 3 of these specimens also contained amphibian remains, however.

***Reproduction***   Presumably similar to that of other bullsnake subspecies.

***Coloring/scale form***   Fewer than 40 irregularly shaped chocolate dorsal saddles ordinarily mark the posterior three quarters of the back, although a pair of Louisiana pine snakes maintained at the Lufkin Zoo vary markedly in coloration. The male, taken from the western edge of the range in the Angelina National Forest, has a grayish-tan crown, a dark masking line through its eyes and across its forehead, a light brown dorsal ground color, and a black crossbarred tail much like that of a bullsnake; the female, from Newton County on the Louisiana border, is an almost uniformly brown serpent whose dark brown dorsal mottling obscures the vertebral saddles and extends to both crown and tail. The belly is white or pale yellow, with brown or black spots along its sides. The central rows of the 28 or more midbody rows of dorsal scales are heavily keeled, there are 4 prefrontal scales, and, as an aid to burrowing, the rostral scale is enlarged and pointed. The anal plate is undivided.

**Similar snakes**   Called pine snakes in the East, bullsnakes in the Midwest, and gopher snakes in the West, all members of the single species *melanoleucus* are similar in body configuration and general marking, though the Louisiana pine's dark-mottled anterior coloring sets it off from the **bullsnake (50)**, defined by its more than 40 dark vertebral squares, distinctly defined as far forward as the nape. Adult **Texas rat snakes (39)** lack the pine snake's crossbanded tail and have only 2 prefrontal scales and a divided anal plate. The **Great Plains rat snake (41)**, which also has but the 2 conventional prefrontal scales and a divided anal plate, is distinguished as well by the dark-bordered, spearpoint-shaped marking on its gray crown.

**Behavior**   Before the sawmills moved into East Texas during the 1920's, Louisiana pine snakes were evidently quite common, attracting frequent written comment for their large size and the dramatic defensive sham in which they would rear the forebody well off the ground while hissing loudly enough to be heard for several yards.

# Sonoran Gopher Snake

*Pituophis melanoleucus affinis*

**Nonvenomous**   See bullsnake (50).

**Abundance**   Common throughout the western United States, *P. m. affinis* is seldom seen in Texas because its range extends into only the western tip of the state.

**Size**   Adults are usually around 3½ feet long, although at 92 inches the record specimen is more than twice that length.

**Habitat**   This subspecies' Texas habitat includes shortgrass prairie, shrub and succulent desert flats, and barren mountain slopes.

**Prey**   With its more easterly relatives, the gopher snake seems to prefer mammalian prey, primarily rodents (especially pocket gophers) and young rabbits; lizards and the eggs and young of ground-nesting birds are also taken. Burrow-dwelling rodents are located by scent, and in ground squirrel colonies gopher snakes often simply take up residence.

**Reproduction**   Reproduction is similar to that of the bullsnake (50).

**Coloring/scale form**   Coloration is generally a bit lighter than that of most *sayi*, with more than 45 big, reddish-brown rectangles spaced along the spine between similar-sized golden brown blocks. The throat is white, shading to pale yellow at midbody; scattered dark spots tip the outer edges of the posterior ventral scales. Four prefrontal scales back the broad, flat, or only slightly raised rostral, the 29 or more midbody rows of dorsal scales are heavily keeled along the spine, and the anal plate is undivided.

**Similar snakes**   The rostral scale of the **bullsnake (50)** is narrower (higher than it is wide) and raised above the adjacent scales. (Of 15 Guadalupe Mountains *Pituophis*, 8 had bullsnake-type rostral scales, 5 were intermediate between *sayi* and *affinis*, and 2 were clearly Sonoran gopher snakes.)

**Behavior**   Large size, diurnal foraging, and slow gait make the adult gopher snake ill suited for either flight or concealment, leaving it with a dramatic hostile posturing as a principal defensive strategy: by raising its forebody, puffing its neck, and fiercely vibrating its tail, a large individual can present as intimidating a facade as a diamondback. Contributing to this lethal-sounding performance is the fin of throat cartilage that protects the front of the airway from the passage of ingested prey animals; when the gopher snake expends its hisses, this buzzes a glottal raspberry in the outgoing airstream.

# Texas Glossy Snake

*Arizona elegans arenicola*

**Nonvenomous**   Large individuals may bite if molested.

**Abundance**   South of Falfurrias and Hebbronville, *A. e. arenicola* is one of the more abundant serpents encountered on warm spring and early summer nights; elsewhere in the state it is very uncommon.

**Size**   Adults are most often 20 to 30 inches in length and rarely grow longer than 3 feet. Recorded to 54⅝ inches.

**Habitat**   Primarily sandy-soiled (*arenicola* means "sand-loving"), thorn-brush-covered portions of the lower Rio Grande plain; occasionally the lower Brazos Valley and the north central Cross Timbers.

**Prey**   Mainly whiptail, racerunner, and spiny lizards scented out after dark while they sleep, as well as small mammalian prey.

**Reproduction**   Egg-bearing. In September and early October up to 2 dozen young, 9½ to 11 inches in length, emerge from the buried clutches of approximately 2⅜-inch-long eggs.

**Coloring/scale form**   The definitive marking unique to glossy snakes is the pale longitudinal line that runs along the spine just behind the head. Forty-one to 60 (average 50) large brown vertebral blotches have very thin dark borders. The smooth dorsal scales, which reflect the nacreous patina suggested by the common name, are arranged in 29 to 35 (average 32) rows at midbody; there are 2 prefrontal scales (see illustration at bullsnake [50]); the belly is white, the anal plate undivided.

**Similar snakes**   **Kansas glossy snakes (54)** generally have slightly less distinct dorsolateral patterning, as well as both statistically more numerous dorsal blotches (41 to 69, average 55) and fewer dorsal scale rows (29 to 31, average 30). **Bullsnakes (50)** are diurnal reptiles that have keeled dorsal scales, laterally speckled bellies, 4 prefrontal scales, and an enlarged rostral. *Pituophis* also lack a pale longitudinal stripe along the nape and have brown-speckled crowns considerably lighter in hue than their backs. **Prairie kingsnakes (43)** also lack a light line along the anterior spine and have big, dark brown squares on their bellies. The **Great Plains rat snake (41)** also lacks the glossy's pale vertebral neck stripe and has a brown spearpoint-shaped marking on its light gray crown, as well as keeled vertebral scales, a partially spotted belly with a longitudinally light-and-dark-striped undertail, and a divided anal plate. The **Texas night snake (83)** has a big chocolate blotch on either side of its neck, an irregularly shaped *dark* vertebral bar or blotch just posterior to its crown, and a divided anal plate.

**Behavior**   Almost never seen above ground except at night.

*LARGE, BROWN-BLOTCHED TERRESTRIAL SNAKES*

# Kansas Glossy Snake

*Arizona elegans elegans*

Northwest of a line through Del Rio, San Saba, and Gainesville, the Texas glossy is replaced by its western plains and Chihuahuan Desert subspecies, *Arizona elegans elegans*. (*Arizona* is Latin for "dry land"; *elegans* refers to this animal's presumably tasteful patterning.) Though perhaps a bit larger on the average (adults range from 20 to 47 inches in length), the Kansas glossy is similar to the Texas in its behavior, scalation, reproductive cycle, and predominantly sandy-soil habitat. Prey is also similar: kangaroo and pocket mice, side-blotched and earless lizards. Although widespread, *A. e. elegans* is evidently but spottily distributed, since its abundance seems to vary radically from place to place: Jameson and Flury's exhaustive West Texas fieldwork (Texas Journal of Science 1 [2]:54–79, 1949) failed to yield a single Kansas glossy, yet 18 years later *A. e. elegans* was more numerous than any other snake collected by McKinney and Ballinger (Southwestern Naturalist 11 [3]:410–12, 1966) in the lower Panhandle. Frederick Gehlbach of Baylor University found it to be not uncommon in the shrub desert around the Guadalupe Mountains, moreover, and Abilene Zoo director Jack Joy reports that large individuals with a faintly pinkish ground color and olive-brown dorsal blotches are found fairly regularly to the northwest of Tom Green County. The Kansas race is distinguished from its southeasterly subspecies, *A. e. arenicola*, by its slightly more numerous (41 to 69, average 55) vertebral blotches and its lower number of dorsal scale rows (29 to 31 at midbody, average 30). Characteristics that distinguish it from other similar snakes are the same as for the Texas glossy (53).

# Painted Desert Glossy Snake

*Arizona elegans philipi*

El Paso County and a bit of western Hudspeth County harbor animals found nowhere else in Texas, in part because of the stretch of dunes that begins here and reaches southward into Mexico, giving rise to a biotic community that includes such sand-adapted animals as the Apache pocket mouse and the most westerly of Texas' glossy snakes, *Arizona elegans philipi*. The Painted Desert glossy—the subspecies name honors Philip M. Klauber, who defined the form in 1946—is similar to the state's 2 more easterly glossy snakes in most respects, and in places other than the West Texas dunes its preferred habitat is similar to theirs, consisting mostly of creosote- and black-brush-covered slopes, sagebrush flats, and sandy-soil grassland. The Painted Desert glossy's nocturnally surface-foraging, diurnally subterranean activity cycle, as well as its reproductive behavior, size, and usual prey, also parallels that of *arenicola* and *elegans*. In addition to its usual 27 dorsal scale rows, *A. e. philipi* differs from more eastern glossy snake races by having a higher number of body blotches (average 64.2) and a relatively long tail (about 15 percent of its total length). Like many arid-land reptiles, *A. e. philipi* is paler than its eastern relatives and lacks their well-defined dark mask, although a faint umber line running from its eye to the corner of its jaw suggests this marking. Also, in this subspecies the golden brown dorsal blotches are often compressed over the spine into a waisted, hourglass shape.

*LARGE, BROWN-BLOTCHED TERRESTRIAL SNAKES*

# Speckled Kingsnake

*Lampropeltis getulus holbrooki*

☐ *Area of intergradation*

***Nonvenomous***   Since this pale yellow- or white-speckled reptile is so clearly different from the blotched or banded pit vipers, it is often picked up—at which point it may bite with determination.

***Abundance***   Seasonally abundant, especially in East Texas and along the upper coast during early spring.

***Size***   Recorded to 6 feet, adults are most often 18 to 36 inches long.

***Habitat***   A variety of microenvironments are inhabited, among them damp, grassy pastures and shelter beneath piles of barrier-beach driftwood and logs and stumps in forested bottomland.

***Prey***   Powerful constrictors, speckled kingsnakes are generalized carnivores on smaller vertebrates, foraging mostly at night (guided by their keen sense of smell), for *Lampropeltis* are too slow-moving to capture most diurnal prey animals during their periods of activity.

***Reproduction***   Egg-bearing. *Getulus* kingsnakes follow a typical serpentine schedule of spring (and perhaps autumn) mating, early summer egg-laying, and late summer hatching. See desert kingsnake (57).

***Coloring/scale form***   Each shiny black or chocolate-colored scale on the rounded crown and thick, tubular neck and trunk bears a dab of pale yellow or white; among juveniles—which appear to be even more profusely light-freckled than the adults because their scales are smaller—many of these spots are clumped together in pale lines that cross the back. The belly is yellow, checkered or blotched with black; the dorsal scales are smooth and arranged in 21 to 23 rows at midbody; and the anal plate is undivided.

***Similar snakes***   In a north-south band ranging in width from 50 miles at the coast to nearly 300 miles along the Red River and eastern Panhandle, the speckled king occupies an overlapping range with its western subspecies, *L. g. splendida*. Although some of *splendida*'s characteristics are evident among most speckled kings in this zone, the typical **desert king (57)** is distinguished by its predominantly blackish belly and crown, its 23 to 25 dorsal scale rows, and its large black or dark brown vertebral saddles. The **buttermilk racer (67)** has much larger pale dorsolateral spots, each of which occupies an entire scale, a neck considerably slimmer than its angular head, an unmarked pale belly, 17 rows of dorsal scales, and a divided anal plate.

***Behavior***   Unlike the dominance combat of rattlers, coachwhips, and bullsnakes (during which the participants' forebodies are reared aggressively off the ground), speckled kings' more deliberate physical rivalries consist of trying merely to crawl or lie on top of each other, which may result in a horizontal spiraling of the trunks while the heads vie for the upper position.

# Desert Kingsnake

*Lampropeltis getulus splendida*

☐ *Area of intergradation*

***Nonvenomous*** Even when confronted with a human predator many times its size, the desert king may put on a valiant defensive display by drawing the neck into an S-curve, vibrating the tail tip, and striking openmouthed. Although large specimens can bite with conviction, the strikes are largely bluff, and the fear-threat response of most individuals consists mainly of defecation and the discharge of odorous musk.

***Abundance*** Despite its name, the desert kingsnake is not a true arid-land animal and is most abundant in the thorn brush of South Texas. Its range also includes extensive mountainous areas west of the Pecos River, but it is not abundant there.

***Size*** Adults average 22 to 38 inches in length; the record is 60 inches.

***Habitat*** A frequently subterranean creature vulnerable (in part because of its slow gait) above ground to predators such as owls, coyotes, skunks, and, in the Rio Grande brush country, bands of snake-eating javelinas.

***Prey*** Most often snakes, lizards, and small mammals, but also clutches of reptile eggs detected beneath the surface by smell.

***Reproduction*** Egg-bearing. After spring breeding, the 5 to 12 adhesive-surfaced eggs are laid in late June or July, sometimes buried as deeply as a foot in search of sufficient humidity to prevent drying through their moisture-permeable shells. The brightly yellow-speckled hatchlings, as glossy and colorful as porcelain figurines, are 8½ to 10 inches in length and weigh about ⅕ ounce. Juveniles often have both poorly defined dorsal saddles and a lateral row of large dark brown spots; as they mature, these spots are first surrounded, then gradually fragmented, by encroaching yellow flecks.

***Coloring/scale form*** The belly of both adult and young is black, with pale blotches marking the outer ends of the ventral plates. The smooth, glossy dorsal scales are arranged in 23 to 25 midbody rows; the anal plate is undivided.

*SPECKLED KINGSNAKES*

***Similar snakes*** Throughout the middle of the state, the ranges of the desert kingsnake and the **speckled king (56)** overlap, producing individuals with characteristics of both subspecies. In pure form, however, the speckled king is distinguished by its uniformly yellow- or white-spotted body and head, as well as its black-blotched yellow belly and 21 to 23 rows of dorsal scales. The very rare **Central American speckled racer (69)** of the lower Rio Grande Valley also lacks dark dorsal saddles and has 17 midbody rows of vertebrally keeled scales, a plain yellow belly, and a divided anal plate. Color phases of the **Texas longnose snake (88)** that lack rectangular red vertebral saddles still have a protruding brown snout and an off-white belly notable for the single row of undertail scales just posterior to the vent (kingsnakes and all other indigenous nonvenomous serpents have a double row of such scales).

***Behavior*** In part because of their thickly muscled bodies, which are resistant to the effects of pit viper venom, desert kingsnakes are indefatigable predators on other serpents: at even the scent of *L. getulus*, quite large rattlers edge backward, attempting to shield their heads with a loop of the trunk.

# Eastern Coachwhip
## Masticophis flagellum flagellum

**Nonvenomous**  If caught or cornered, coachwhips will bite aggressively, leaving long, shallow scratches.

**Abundance**  The most common large terrestrial serpent in much of its range.

**Size**  The record eastern coachwhip measured 8½ feet in length, but an individual this size would be almost as unusual as an 8-foot-tall human being: the majority of adult *M. f. flagellum* are between 3½ and 5½ feet long.

**Habitat**  Coachwhips occur in virtually every dry rural community, but *M. flagellum* seems to be particularly abundant around abandoned farms.

**Prey**  Texas spiny and tree lizards probably compose much of the diet, although other snakes, mammals, birds, frogs, baby turtles, and insects are also taken.

**Reproduction**  Egg-bearing. Eleven to 16 inches in length, the hatchlings are first seen in late August and September and are colored so differently from the adults—with brown anterior dorsal crossbars on a tan ground hue and cream-colored bellies anteriorly spotted with a double row of black dots—that in spite of the large eyes, pronounced supraocular scales, slender bodies, and crosshatched tails they share with their parents, they are frequently assumed to belong to another species.

**Coloring/scale form**  Adult *M. f. flagellum* exhibit a unique two-toned color combination: the predominantly unmarked dark forebody fades posteriorly to progressively lighter shades of brown and tan—even the entirely black individuals found between Liberty and Texarkana have reddish-tinted tails—while the smooth scales' slightly darker borders create on the posterior body a faintly crosshatched, braided-whiplike pattern. See western coachwhip (59).

The head is also distinctive: narrow, angular, and elongate (yet wider than the wiry neck), with big eyes shielded above by projecting scale plates and bordered along their forward edges by a pair of small preocular scales. The dorsal scales are arranged in 17 rows at midbody (13 just ahead of the vent), and the anal plate is divided.

*WHIPSNAKES, RACERS, AND INDIGO SNAKES*

**Similar snakes** Across a wide strip from Brazoria County on the coast to Wichita County on the Red River, the ranges of eastern and **western coachwhips (59)** overlap, with the latter being distinguished primarily by its more uniform (anterior to posterior), lighter beige to brownish dorsolateral color, often barred with wide light or dark crossbands. Its belly resembles that of the juvenile eastern coachwhip: creamy, with a double row of dark dots beneath the neck. **Southern black (66)** and **eastern yellowbelly (64) racers** lack the eastern coachwhip's dark-anterior, lighter-posterior coloring, as well as its crosshatched tail; racers also have 15 rows of dorsal scales just ahead of the vent.

**Behavior** Coachwhips can both traverse open ground more swiftly than any other North American serpent and, especially when pursued, climb rapidly into densely branched low trees.

# Western Coachwhip
## *Masticophis flagellum testaceus*

**Nonvenomous**   Western coachwhips are agile biters that may strike past a human assailant's hands at his face or body.

**Abundance**   Probably the most common large, nonvenomous serpent in terrestrial rural environments throughout its range.

**Size**   The young are 12 to 14 inches long at hatching; most adults measure between 4 and 5½ feet. The record is 6 feet 8 inches.

**Habitat**   Almost every dryland, nonurban habitat in western Texas.

**Prey**   A generalized hunter that as an adult feeds on a variety of mostly vertebrate prey; the young also eat insects.

**Reproduction**   Egg-bearing. See eastern coachwhip (58). The tan young are dimly crossbarred with brown, mainly across the neck and anterior trunk.

**Coloring/scale form**   Often reflecting the general cast of its home terrain, *M. f. testaceus'* coloration is lighter among more westerly populations, but its head and neck are always slightly darker than its trunk and tail. On the gray limestone of the Edwards Plateau, entirely silvery tan coachwhips predominate, while west of the Pecos River, many have rosy brown forebodies or are brick red above; some also have broad light and dark dorsolateral crossbands. The belly is creamy gray, with at least the anterior ventral scales marked by a double row of black spots.

 *M. flagellum*'s most distinctive characteristic, however, is the light-dark crosshatch patterning of its tail. Since each dorsal caudal scale is two-toned—the forward portion is paler than its trailing edge—the coachwhip's posterior body has the look of a braided buggy whip, although its scales are actually quite smooth. They are arranged in 17 rows at midbody (13 rows just in front of the vent), the anal plate is divided, and a unique pair of lorilabial scales—the lower one very small—borders the anterior edge of the eye.

**Similar snakes**   The range of the **eastern coachwhip (58)** shades into that of the western race along a line running from Brazoria County on the coast to Wichita County on the Oklahoma border; it has uniformly dark foreparts with a lighter brown posterior trunk and tail that is reddish on otherwise all-black East Texas individuals. **Eastern yellowbelly (64)** and **Mexican (65) racers** lack both the coachwhip's crosshatched tail and its beige to rust to light gray dorsal hue; racers also have 15 rows of dorsal scales just ahead of the vent. **Whipsnakes (60–63)** are slenderer serpents with thin white lateral markings, reddish undertails, and 15 midbody rows of dorsal scales.

**Behavior**   Its mostly open-terrain diurnal foraging renders *M. flagellum* vulnerable to predation by carnivorous birds, and red-tailed hawks are often seen sitting on power line poles with these snakes dangling from their talons; juveniles also fall prey to roadrunners.

*WHIPSNAKES, RACERS, AND INDIGO SNAKES*

# Central Texas Whipsnake

*Masticophis taeniatus girardi*

**Nonvenomous**   This high-strung animal is likely to thrash about and bite lightly if restrained.

**Abundance**   Common, especially in the Trans-Pecos. Because of the thick, brushy cover they inhabit in the eastern portion of their range, whipsnakes are relatively unfamiliar reptiles even to rural human residents of their habitat.

**Size**   Despite their considerable length—adult size is 28 to 72 inches—these reptiles are so slender that even the largest individuals have heads no bigger than a man's thumb: one healthy 3½-footer weighed but 5.6 ounces.

**Habitat**   Oak-juniper evergreen woodland in Central Texas; in the Trans-Pecos, dry watercourses and brushy riverbanks, barren, rocky situations up to 6,000 feet in elevation, and evergreen mountain woodland.

**Prey**   Lizards, snakes, and small rodents; the young probably also take insects.

**Reproduction**   Egg-bearing; see desert striped whipsnake (61). The 12- to 15-inch-long young are colored much like their parents except that the pale band across the nape is more pronounced, while a white lateral stripe—not yet broken into the elongate patches typical of the adult—occupies the third and fourth scale rows above the belly.

**Coloring/scale form**   Variable. Among Central Texas specimens an unbroken row of tiny white flecks generally marks both the lowest of the 15 midbody rows of smooth, blackish dorsal scales and the outer tips of the gray-and-white-mottled belly plates, which, posterior to the divided anal plate, shade to pink. In West Texas, individuals may fit this description, have brownish dorsolateral crossbands, or even be predominantly mahogany above, with charcoal anterior bellies.

***Similar snakes***  Throughout the northern Trans-Pecos, this serpent inter-grades with its subspecies the **desert striped whipsnake (61),** which in pure form is distinguished by its dark gray-brown to rusty dorsolateral coloring and by the pair of thin white seams that lines each side from nose to tail tip (the uppermost of these is longitudinally split by a blackish streak, the lower touches the outer edge of the belly). Along the southeastern edge of the Edwards Plateau, the Central Texas race also intergrades with its more south-erly subspecies, the **Schott's whipsnake (62)**—a race distinguished by its bluish-olive posterior dorsal coloration, the pair of whitish lines along its sides, and the orangish flecks often found on the lower portion of its neck and anterior sides. The **western coachwhip (59)** lacks a pale lateral stripe; 17 rows of dorsal scales cover its anterior trunk.

***Behavior***  Whipsnakes are among the most radically shaped of serpents, ap-parent reptilian greyhounds whose wiry configuration is instead principally adaptive to resisting heat and desiccation, allowing them to forage during the hottest part of the day, when their lizard prey is most active.

# Desert Striped Whipsnake

*Masticophis taeniatus taeniatus*

**Nonvenomous**   Nervous, fragile animals, whipsnakes, if cornered or seized, typically defend themselves with superficial nips.

**Abundance**   Desert striped whipsnakes are locally common in West Texas uplands such as the Guadalupe Mountains.

**Size**   Most adults measure 30 to 61 inches in length.

**Habitat**   Both rocky succulent desert and evergreen mountain woodland at elevations up to 7,000 feet.

**Prey**   Primarily lizards and snakes—small western diamondback rattlers have been reported—as well as rodents, nestling birds, and insects.

**Reproduction**   Egg-bearing. Like other *M. taeniatus*, this subspecies lays clutches of 3 to 12 relatively large, slightly rough-surfaced eggs; the hatchlings emerge in early autumn and are no thicker than a pencil.

**Coloring/scale form**   Ventral coloring is mottled gray and white below the forebody, shading to coral beneath the tail. The dorsal scales are smooth, arranged in 15 rows at midbody, and the anal plate is divided.

**Similar snakes**   As with other whipsnakes, the desert striped intergrades with any race of *M. taeniatus* whose range abuts its own; throughout the northern Trans-Pecos, this merging involves the **Central Texas whipsnake (60),** which in typical form is distinguished by its black back broken only by white neck patches and the row of long white dashes along its anterior sides. **Western coachwhips (59)** are larger than whipsnakes and are generally pale dorsally; they have 17 dorsal scale rows at midbody and lack white lateral lines.

**Behavior**   Whipsnakes' thin bodies afford such effective camouflage that these animals are able virtually to disappear by freezing motionless, which renders their narrow profiles as inconspicuous as plant stems.

# Schott's Whipsnake
*Masticophis taeniatus schotti*

**Nonvenomous**   Like other whipsnakes, the Schott's will nip if it is molested.

**Abundance**   In Duval, Brooks, Jim Wells, Kleberg, and Kenedy counties these animals are seasonally abundant.

**Size**   Most often Schott's whipsnakes are 40 to 56 inches long—the largest example on record measured 66 inches—although adults are not much thicker than a fountain pen and weigh only a few ounces.

**Habitat**   The coastal plain southeast of the Balcones Fault: both grassland punctuated with mesquite and prickly pear and the Tamaulipan thorn brush of catclaw acacia, paloverde, tamarisk, cenizo, and ocotillo that prevails where agriculture has not leveled the Rio Grande plain's native growth.

**Prey**   Fast-moving small animals such as racerunner lizards instantly attract this reptile's attention and are swiftly pursued, grasped with the jaws, and, if too large to be immediately engulfed, pressed against the ground by a loop of the trunk; as with other whipsnakes, snakes and small rodents are also taken, while the young often feed on insects.

**Reproduction**   Egg-bearing. Three Texas clutches laid in May and June consisted of 3, 10, and 12 rough-surfaced eggs, each about 1½ inches long. Hatchlings reportedly sometimes have a reddish cast on their foreparts.

**Coloring/scale form**   The underside is whitish or cream-colored beneath the chin, stippled with bluish gray farther to the rear, then deep yellow to salmon below the tail. The dorsal scales are smooth and arranged in 15 rows at midbody; the anal plate is divided.

**Similar snakes**   Schott's whipsnake intergrades in at least 2 areas; along the southeastern Edwards Plateau its distribution overlaps that of the Central Texas race, while its genetic influence is evident among Ruthven's whipsnakes throughout the lower Rio Grande Valley. The typical **Central Texas whipsnake (60)** is dark brown or black above, with prominent white patches across its nape and a series of white dashes along its anterior sides; it lacks the Schott's pair of continuous white dorsolateral lines. **Ruthven's whipsnake (63)** is greener, often lacks the distinct white side stripes of the Schott's, and has gray or dark orange spots on its otherwise bright yellow throat, as well as a bright red undertail.

**Western coachwhips (59)** are more robustly proportioned serpents, never dull blue-green in color. They lack *M. taeniatus'* lateral striping and have 17 rows of dorsal scales at midbody.

**Behavior**   Like other whipsnakes and racers, *M. t. schotti* is a curious animal that investigates any unusual activity within its territory, punctuating its erratic, darting movements with sudden starts and stops.

*WHIPSNAKES, RACERS, AND INDIGO SNAKES*

# Ruthven's Whipsnake

*Masticophis taeniatus ruthveni*

**Nonvenomous**   *M. t. ruthveni* is active, nervous, and quick both to flee and to nip in its own defense.

**Abundance**   Formerly common throughout the Rio Grande Valley, Ruthven's whipsnake is now abundant only in the small area of mesquite savannah and thorn woodland that remains in this region.

**Size**   The usual adult length is 40 to 56 inches; the record is 66⅛ inches.

**Habitat**   At one time this animal probably occurred throughout the Tamaulipan brush country of northern Mexico and South Texas.

**Prey**   Similar to that of Texas' other whipsnake subspecies: a variety of small vertebrate animals, especially lizards and smaller snakes.

**Reproduction**   Egg-bearing. See Schott's whipsnake (62). Juveniles have a black-edged pale side stripe on the adjacent portions of the third and fourth scale rows above the belly but lack the adults' light anterior vertebral scale margins as well as most of their dark belly stippling.

**Coloring/scale form**   The leading edge of some of the anterior vertebral scales is cream-colored, shading to olive, or sometimes reddish gray, toward the tail. The sides are slightly lighter in hue than the back and may be faintly marked behind the jaw with rusty orange spots, while the pale yellow forebelly changes to blue-gray lightly mottled with salmon on the middle third of the belly, then becomes pink toward the vent and red on the undersurface of the tail. The smooth dorsal scales occur in 15 rows at midbody; the anal plate is divided.

**Similar snakes**   North of the Rio Grande, virtually all *M. t. ruthveni* are intergrade animals that exhibit characteristics of the **Schott's whipsnake (62),** from which they differ mainly in either possessing much less conspicuous white side stripes, confined to the neck and forebody, or lacking them altogether. The Ruthven's yellowish anterior belly and red undertail also differ from the Schott's whitish forebelly and salmon undertail. The **Mexican racer (65)** is less wiry in shape, lacks the whipsnake's ventral stippling and thin white side stripes, and has 17 midbody dorsal scale rows. The dark gray to silvery brown **western coachwhip (59)** also has 17 anterior rows of smooth dorsal scales, lacks lateral stripes, and has a faintly defined braided or crosshatched scale pattern on its tail.

**Behavior**   Much of *M. t. ruthveni*'s U.S. habitat has been lost to agricultural and residential development, although this animal is still numerous along the coast in Cameron County; in behavior and natural history it is presumably similar to other whipsnake subspecies.

# Eastern Yellowbelly Racer

*Coluber constrictor flaviventris*

**Nonvenomous**   C. c. *flaviventris* will bite in self-defense if cornered or grasped. It is unable to inflict more than scratches, but captives almost never resign themselves to being handled.

**Abundance**   The most numerous and widely distributed of its genus in the state, the eastern yellowbelly is known in many rural areas as the blue racer.

**Size**   Although reported to reach nearly 6 feet in length, adults are generally between 30 and 54 inches long.

**Habitat**   Mostly woodland-meadow interface (eastern yellowbelly racers seem to avoid dense forest), as well as weed-grown fields and the vicinity of derelict buildings where boards and fallen sheets of metal siding provide shelter; in open grassland this reptile may coil under bushes or clumps of bunchgrass or inhabit rocky ledges along watercourses.

**Prey**   Insects make up the largest percentage of animals consumed, but C. c. *flaviventris* will generally eat any small creature it can capture, including rodents, ground-nesting birds and their eggs, lizards, frogs, and smaller snakes.

**Reproduction**   Egg-bearing. During the breeding season in April and May, male racers become quite aggressive, with several sometimes courting a single female. Laid during June, July, and early August in a variety of places—within the tunnels of small burrowing mammals, beneath rotting boards or sheets of iron siding, and in loose soil along the margins of plowed fields—the 3 to 23 yellowish-white, rough-surfaced eggs measure up to 1⅝ inches in length. The young, which hatch in 43 to 63 days, are between 9 and 12 inches long and are active hunters whose brown-blotched dorsal coloring is entirely different from the unmarked olive backs of their parents. (The hatchlings' dark vertebral saddles, big, yellow-irised eyes, and 17 anterior rows of dorsal scales set them off from adults of the similar-sized burrowing serpents found in the same leaf-litter microenvironment, however.)

**Coloring/scale form**   By the time they reach 16 inches in length, during their second year, young racers have begun to lose their juvenile pattern. Beginning on the tail, the back gradually fades into a solid olive-brown as the chin, throat, belly, and lower sides exchange their dark juvenile spots for the unmarked cream or yellow of the adult. Seventeen rows of smooth dorsal scales line the middle of the trunk (15 just ahead of the vent), there are usually 7 upper labials, and the anal plate is divided.

*WHIPSNAKES, RACERS, AND INDIGO SNAKES*

**Similar snakes**  Over much of Trans-Pecos Texas the eastern yellowbelly intergrades with the **Mexican racer (65),** a more southerly and westerly subspecies with an often slightly darker vertebral line, paler, more greenish sides, and 8 upper labial scales. **Eastern (58)** and **western (59) coachwhips** have a distinctive, braided-looking scale pattern on the posterior body and tail as well as 13 rows of dorsal scales across the trunk just ahead of the vent.

**Behavior**  Most eastern yellowbelly racers occupy relatively well-defined ranges of around 25 acres; only a few have been known to travel as far as ¾ mile. Their active, diurnal foraging renders them susceptible to avian carnivores, and throughout most of this reptile's range even large individuals fall prey to hawks and roadrunners.

# Mexican Racer

*Coluber constrictor oaxaca*

**Nonvenomous**   Like other *Coluber constrictor*, this snake will nip vigorously if it is unable to escape.

**Abundance**   Fairly common in South Texas, though not often seen because of its elusive habits.

**Size**   Slightly smaller than other Texas racers, most adult *C. c. oaxaca* measure between 20 and 40 inches in length.

**Habitat**   Open woodland interspersed with grassy meadows and scattered brush; this animal may be found coiled in clumps of cactus or hidden under boards and debris around unworked farms, though it also inhabits suburban vacant lots and even city parks. Mexican racers also occur in small relict populations scattered across Trans-Pecos Texas.

**Prey**   Young *C. c. oaxaca* take far more insects (mostly grasshoppers and crickets) than small vertebrate food animals, while the adults also consume rodents, frogs, snakes, and a great many lizards.

**Reproduction**   Egg-bearing. With the approach of their early summer laying period, females tend to congregate in denser vegetation than they frequent at other times, subsequently hiding their 5 to 12 1½-inch-long eggs beneath litter or burying them under a layer of sandy soil. Unlike the young of other Texas racers, which have rounded brown saddles along the spine, juvenile *C. c. oaxaca* are marked with narrower, jagged-edged dark bands across the forward part of the back, flanked by brown flecks scattered over their buff-ground-colored sides; both the crown and the posterior back are grayish brown.

**Coloring/scale form**   A slender, medium-sized colubrid whose adult coloring consists of a uniformly olive-gray back and paler gray-green sides; in some individuals the lateral areas are so much lighter than the back that the snake appears to have a dusky stripe along its spine. Occasional specimens also show dark blue or black skin between the scales—colors that may also appear on the forward edges of the scales themselves. The lips, chin, and belly are yellow or yellowish green, with a few individuals having yellowish-pink throats. Seventeen rows of smooth dorsal scales line the middle of the trunk (15 just anterior to the vent), there are usually 8 upper labial scales, and the anal plate is divided.

*WHIPSNAKES, RACERS, AND INDIGO SNAKES*

**Similar snakes**   Hatchling Mexican racers are distinguished from other mottled little terrestrial serpents by their narrow dorsolateral crossbands and 17 rows of smooth dorsal scales. Among adults, the **eastern yellowbelly racer (64)** has a more uniformly olive-brown back and sides and 7 upper labial scales. The **western coachwhip (59)** is a more robust beige, silvery tan, rusty, or pinkish serpent with a faintly braided or crosshatched caudal scale pattern and 13 rows of dorsal scales just in front of its vent.

**Behavior**   C. c. oaxaca is most evident from May to July, although another seasonal peak of activity occurs in October; foraging is generally divided into morning and afternoon periods, especially when the temperature at these times falls between 70 and 85 degrees Fahrenheit.

# Southern Black Racer

*Coluber constrictor priapus*

**Nonvenomous**   Quick-tempered and likely to strike several times at an aggressor, this subspecies seems to be somewhat more high-strung than the eastern yellowbelly racer (64).

**Abundance**   *Coluber constrictor priapus* occurs only as far west as the northeastern tip of Texas, where it is numerous on brushy terraces along the Red River.

**Size**   Adults are 20 to 56 inches long.

**Habitat**   The preferred habitat in Texas seems to be pine or mixed evergreen-deciduous forest-meadowland interface, especially where there is an abundance of low-level shrubbery.

**Prey**   Southern black racers prey on a variety of small animals from insects and their larvae to vertebrates such as frogs, toads, lizards, snakes, birds and their eggs, and rodents.

**Reproduction**   Egg-bearing. Seven to 18 slightly oval, 1-by-1¾-inch, rough-textured eggs are laid in humid subsurface cavities—a few of which are reportedly used year after year by several females who deposit their clutches in a single communal chamber. The 9- to 14-inch-long hatchlings emerge in July and August. Radically different in appearance from the adults, the cream-ground-colored young are conspicuously patterned with chestnut-brown vertebral saddles that become indistinct as they merge together toward the tail; on the forebody, small brown lateral spots may be paralleled by a line of little dark crescents along the outer margin of the belly.

**Coloring/scale form**   Some white is generally visible on the chin and throat, while the remainder of the belly ranges from pale yellowish gray to as dark a charcoal as the back; the iris of the eye is a distinctive reddish-orange hue. Seventeen rows of smooth dorsal scales occur at midbody (15 just anterior to the vent), and as in other racers, the anal plate is divided.

**Similar snakes**   Even in its black color phase the **eastern coachwhip (58)** has a slightly rusty-hued tail; it also has a dark forebelly and 13 rows of dorsal scales just ahead of the vent.

**Behavior**   During the spring and summer of 1981 several *C. c. priapus* were observed to maintain fairly well-defined home territories around the rocky outcroppings of grassy, oak-studded hillsides in Grayson County.

*WHIPSNAKES, RACERS, AND INDIGO SNAKES*

# Buttermilk Racer

*Coluber constrictor anthicus*

**Nonvenomous**   C. c. anthicus does not exhibit aggressiveness except in self-defense; even in distress, however, it usually bluffs by striking openmouthed and seldom actually bites down.

**Abundance**   Fairly common: during one week in mid-May 9 specimens were found on the grounds of a Lake Houston golf course.

**Size**   Most adults are 30 to 60 inches long and rather slender; the record is 70 inches.

**Habitat**   Buttermilk racers favor overgrown fields, meadows, or partially open areas at the edge of forests, where they shelter in brier patches or brushy undergrowth.

**Prey**   In the single study of this subspecies' diet, mice were found in the stomachs of 25 adult specimens, rats were discovered in 5, lizards in 8, frogs in 7, and birds in 3.

**Reproduction**   Egg-bearing. Of 3 clutches deposited at the Houston Zoo between May 25 and 29, 2 consisted of 18, the third of 27, slightly rough-surfaced eggs just over an inch long; most hatched 46 days later into 10- to 11-inch-long young. Juvenile dorsal patterning is similar to that of the closely related eastern yellowbelly (64), tan (68), and southern black (66) racers: a cream ground color is blotched with brown vertebral saddles and small, chocolate-colored lateral spots.

**Coloring/scale form**   The dorsal ground color is generally dark bluish or greenish gray on the foreparts, lighter and browner to the rear, especially where the buttermilk's range merges with that of the subspecies tan racer. A dense spattering of entirely off-white scales is usually present, but these are scattered and few in number on some individuals; intergrades with the lighter-hued tan racer may exhibit a long, white-spotted dark patch on their napes. The lips, chin, and lower sides of the neck are yellow, while the belly is light gray, often with a few pale yellow spots. The dorsal scales are smooth and arranged, like those of all racers, in 17 rows at midbody and 15 rows just forward of the vent; the anal plate is divided.

**Similar snakes**   North of Liberty, in Angelina, Polk, Tyler, and northern Jasper and Newton counties, as the buttermilk begins to intergrade with its subspecies the **tan racer (68),** the dark, pale-spotted dorsolateral ground color of C. c. anthicus begins to fade, first on the posterior trunk, into the lighter, more brownish hue of C. c. etheridgei. The **speckled kingsnake (56)** is a heavier-bodied, slower-moving blackish serpent peppered with tiny pale dots; its yellow belly is blotched with black, and its anal plate is undivided.

**Behavior**   Similar to that of other Texas racers.

# Tan Racer
*Coluber constrictor etheridgei*

**Nonvenomous**   *C. c. etheridgei* will bite to defend itself but is unable to inflict more than scratches.

**Abundance**   Apparently not uncommon within its very limited range.

**Size**   From 8 to 12 inches at hatching, this subspecies has been recorded to nearly 6 feet in length; most adults measure 3 to 5 feet, however.

**Habitat**   Unlike most other Texas racers, which prefer more open country, *etheridgei* is predominantly a forest-dweller, living among dense stands of never-timbered longleaf pine. As this mature forest habitat has been progressively eliminated, the resulting cut-over areas have been invaded by the more open- or brushy-terrain-living buttermilk racer (67), whose range now completely surrounds that of *etheridgei*.

**Prey**   Predatory behavior is similar to that of other East Texas racers.

**Reproduction**   Egg-bearing. The only extant data are that on May 28, a female from east of Woodville in Tyler County laid 30 eggs, each a little more than an inch long, at the Houston Zoo. Hatchling racers are distinguished from other small terrestrial serpents with brown dorsolateral patterning by their dark vertebral saddles, their proportionately large heads and yellow eyes, and their singular combination of a divided anal plate and 17 rows of smooth dorsal scales at midbody, 15 just ahead of the vent.

**Coloring/scale form**   Variable. This subspecies may be almost uniformly tan, randomly flecked with the pale dorsolateral scales it shares with East Texas' more widespread, dark-backed form, the buttermilk racer, or patterned only with a white-spotted patch of dark bluish or greenish gray on its nape. The belly of both adult and juvenile is unmarked light gray, with some yellowish spots. As with all *Coluber constrictor*, the trunk is long and slender, the head angular; the dorsal scales are smooth, with a maximum of 17 dorsal rows at midbody (15 just anterior to the vent), and the anal plate is divided.

**Similar snakes**   The **buttermilk racer (67)** is similar, except for its dark gray-blue or gray-green back and much more profuse dorsolateral infusion of off-white scales. Intergrades between the two (with darker forebodies and paler, brownish tails) are common. The **speckled kingsnake (56)** is a heavier-bodied, much slower-moving, mostly nocturnal, blackish reptile whose back and sides are uniformly peppered with tiny pale dots; its yellow belly is blotched with black and its anal plate is undivided.

**Behavior**   This reptile's habits and natural history are probably nearly the same as those of other Texas racers.

# Central American Speckled Racer

*Drymobius margaritiferus*
*margaritiferus*

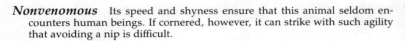

**Nonvenomous**   Its speed and shyness ensure that this animal seldom encounters human beings. If cornered, however, it can strike with such agility that avoiding a nip is difficult.

**Abundance**   The northernmost limit of *D. m. margaritiferus'* range—it is the only member of its genus to reach the United States—lies at the tip of the Rio Grande Valley in Cameron and eastern Hidalgo counties; because of the constantly expanding territorial demands of farmers and real estate developers in this area, it is now among the rarest reptiles in Texas.

**Size**   Adults average 30 to 40 inches; the maximum recorded length is 50 inches.

**Habitat**   The speckled racer prefers dense thickets heavily littered with plant debris, generally near water where its amphibian prey may be found; it has also been found in the handful of Texas-palm groves that remain in Cameron County, despite the fact that these stands seldom retain their natural layered floor of decaying fronds.

**Prey**   Central American speckled racers are diurnal predators on frogs and toads.

**Reproduction**   Egg-bearing. Clutches of 2 to 8 nonadhesive, smooth-shelled whitish eggs, each approximately 1⅝ inches in length and ⅝ inch in diameter, are laid between April and August; emerging after an incubation period of some 8 weeks, the hatchlings are only about 6 inches long. Compared to the adults, they are more vividly colored, with each scale centered with a small white spot.

**Coloring/scale form**   Both juveniles and adults have largely unmarked pale greenish-yellow bellies, although under the tail the ventral plates are bordered with black on their trailing edges. Arranged in 17 rows at midbody, the glossy dorsal scales are weakly keeled along the spine and have apical pits; the anal plate is divided.

**Similar snakes**   **Desert kingsnakes (57)** have big blackish blotches along the spine, entirely smooth dorsal scales, and a predominantly black belly with an undivided anal plate.

**Behavior**   In Guatemala similar *Drymobius* subspecies are abundant in brushy river bottoms, where they constantly search damp places for prey; they are also seen in both open savannah and woodland, as well as in overgrown fields and cleared village back yards.

# Texas
# Indigo
# Snake

*Drymarchon corais erebennus*

***Nonvenomous***   On cool, sunny winter days, when they emerge to bask, indigo snakes appear to be incredibly gentle, letting themselves be handled immediately after capture; when very warm and active, however, some individuals bite vigorously with strong jaws that can inflict deep cuts.

***Abundance***   Because of the widespread conversion of its habitat to agriculture, *D. c. erebennus* is now largely restricted to remnant areas of South Texas' mesquite savannah and thorn brush woodland. (In addition, their great size and diurnal foraging make it so difficult for indigos to escape detection that they are generally quickly exterminated near populated areas.) A considerable population is also present in semidesert as far west as Val Verde County.

***Size***   The longest snake in the state: Texas indigos over 8½ feet in length have been recorded. Most adults are much smaller, however, with adult males averaging 5½ to 6½ feet in length and 4 to 5½ pounds in weight, females about 5 to 5½ feet and 3½ pounds.

***Habitat***   Although it occurs in other environments ranging from grassy prairie to coastal sandhills, *D. c. erebennus* is most plentiful in the thorn brush woodland and mesquite savannah of the coastal plain from Beeville south to the Rio Grande. Here, tree-filled riparian corridors constitute the best microhabitat. (To shed their skins these reptiles seem to require a rather moist milieu—which in arid terrain they find in underground tunnels where the humidity is much higher than at the surface.)

***Prey***   Adult indigos forage rapidly through burrows and across the bare or grassy ground between patches of thorn thicket in search of any vertebrate (including large pit vipers, although they are not the preferred prey) big enough to attract their attention and small enough to be swallowed.

***Reproduction***   Egg-bearing. During the late winter breeding season, the territoriality of adult males waxes to the extent that they sometimes inflict 6-inch-long razorlike fang cuts on each other's foreparts. Fewer than 12 oblong whitish eggs—as much as 3 inches in length and 1.3 inches in diameter, their leathery surfaces covered with fine pebbling—are deposited as early as April; after 70 to 85 days of incubation, the 18- to 26-inch-long hatchlings emerge in midsummer.

*WHIPSNAKES, RACERS, AND INDIGO SNAKES*

***Coloring/scale form*** The belly evidences a singular combination of cloudy orange and blue-gray, with some areas showing more orange, some more gray. Dark facial striping and faint dorsal patterning is evident on some individuals. The 17 midbody rows (14 on the posterior trunk) of big dorsal scales are smooth-surfaced, with a glossy, translucent sheen; the anal plate is undivided.

***Similar snakes*** There are no other terrestrial serpents in South Texas with an entirely black back and sides.

***Behavior*** Most *Drymarchon* are too restless to make satisfactory captives, and, unable to settle into the lethargy that confinement requires, many rub their snouts raw in attempts to pry their way out of their cages. Unlike the arboreal pythons and boas, which soon learn to feel comfortable draped over their keeper's limbs, the terrestrial indigo is ill at ease when held off the ground, and the constant efforts of such individuals to be free of human contact make it evident that they should have been left at large. *Drymarchon* are also very smelly creatures, so given to voiding musk and feces during handling that a truism among herpetologists is that anyone who has maintained one never wants to care for another.

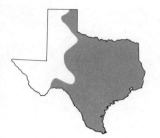

# Diamondback Water Snake

*Nerodia rhombifera rhombifera*

**Nonvenomous**   A vigorous biter with an extraordinary musking ability when molested. This behavior (coupled with its dark, heavy body and aquatic habitat) causes *N. rhombifera* to be consistently mistaken for the cottonmouth, but the majority of "moccasins" found around rural and suburban ponds are actually diamondback, blotched, or yellowbelly water snakes.

**Abundance**   The most common aquatic serpent throughout the coastal plain south of Houston; less abundant in the central and northeastern parts of the state.

**Size**   The record is just over 5 feet, but most adults are 20 to 34 inches long.

**Habitat**   Almost any nonurban body of water in the eastern two thirds of the state (man-made objects left along the banks are a frequent source of shelter), although diamondbacks frequently forage in moist grassland some distance from water.

**Prey**   Varies considerably with locale. Carrion seems to be important, for example, with other food species being divided between frogs and rough fish; few healthy game fish are taken.

**Reproduction**   Live-bearing. Twenty-two litters, all deposited between the first of August and mid-October, averaged 37.3 young 8¼ to 10¼ inches in length.

**Coloring/scale form**   Blackish-brown lines form a diamond-shaped network across the back that intersects dark vertical bars along the sides; the yellowish belly is randomly marked with small blackish crescents. The 25 to 31 midbody rows of dorsal scales are strongly keeled; the anal plate is divided.

*AQUATIC SNAKES*

***Similar snakes*** Water snakes are distinguished from the **western cotton-mouth (97)** by their rounded noses, clearly visible round pupils, and lack of a big dark heat-sensing pit between the eye and the nostril. From anal plate to tail tip water snakes have a double row of belly scales—pit vipers have a single row posterior to the vent—while the cottonmouth's more abruptly tapered tail is also distinctive. Cottonmouths swim more deliberately than water snakes, moreover, undulating slowly, then floating motionless on the surface, while water snakes wriggle steadily forward; if they pause, their bodies sink until only the head is exposed.

Adult **blotched water snakes (72)** have a dim row of pale little vertebral crossbars edged with dark brown and only dimly dark-blocked sides. The blotched's subspecies, the **yellowbelly water snake (73),** has an unmarked dark back and a plain yellow underside. **Green water snakes (77)** have yellowish-white forebellies and gray posterior bellies sprinkled with pale yellow to cinnamon crescents. Their dark, faintly speckled backs and sides lack the diamondback's network of blackish-brown lines, while a row of small subocular scales not found in other *Nerodia* separates the eye from the upper labial scales.

***Behavior*** An unusual predatory strategy involves sensitive lateral areas about a third of the way along the trunk. When these are touched, *N. rhombifera* snaps sideways in an automatic strike response that—in combination with its habit of circling as it swims along pond and river banks after dark— probably increases its chances of seizing prey.

# Blotched Water Snake

## Nerodia erythrogaster transversa

**Nonvenomous**   If unable to escape, this reptile may flatten its head and neck and strike several times in succession. Yet most of its strikes are bluffs, and those that do connect ordinarily result in only a warning nip.

**Abundance**   In the central and west central parts of the state the blotched occurs in lakes, bayous, ponds, rivers, and stock tanks.

**Size**   Most adults are 2 to 3 feet in length; the record is 58 inches.

**Habitat**   The chocolate-blotched newborns are often found in shallower, more dappled microenvironments—both small streams and the inlets of larger bodies of water—than the more uniformly colored adults. (The most westerly *transversa*, which occupy rocky streambed channels, retain distinct dorsal patterning throughout their lives.)

**Prey**   Primarily fish, frogs, tadpoles, and crustaceans.

**Reproduction**   Live-bearing. Breeding takes place on land in spring; the 5 to 27 young—7½ to 10½ inches long and indistinguishable from young yellowbelly water snakes (73)—are born in August and September.

**Coloring/scale form**   Dark-bordered pale bars are generally dimly evident along the spine, while the belly is yellow, with the edges of larger animals' ventral plates lightly tinged with brown. The 23 to 27 midbody rows of dorsal scales are heavily keeled; the anal plate is divided.

**Similar snakes**   The vertically slit pupil of the **western cottonmouth (97)** distinguishes it from the circular pupil of all water snakes; the cottonmouth also has a sizable dark heat-sensing pit between its eye and nostril, and an angular head whose flat, undercut cheeks abruptly intersect its crown. Cottonmouths' tails narrow sharply from their thick posterior bodies (the longer tails of water snakes have a more gradual taper), and among newborn cottonmouths the tail tip is grayish yellow; young water snakes' tails are brown.

   Although intergrades between blotched and **yellowbelly water snakes (73)** occur throughout East Central Texas, the typical yellowbelly is unmarked above, while the posterior edges of the belly scales are a lighter yellow. The **diamondback water snake (71)** has dark vertical bars along its sides that join in rhomboid-shaped links across its back, as well as numerous small black crescents on its belly. **Green water snakes (77)** have yellowish-white foreparts that shade to gray before midbody, where a sprinkling of pale yellow to cinnamon crescents begins. There are no cross-dorsal bars, and a row of small subocular scales separates the upper labials from the eye.

**Behavior**   At times *N. e. transversa* may venture a half-mile or more from water after dark, especially following heavy rainstorms that wash insects to the ground and bring out feeding frogs and toads.

*AQUATIC SNAKES*

# Yellowbelly Water Snake

*Nerodia erythrogaster flavigaster*

**Nonvenomous**   Like its subspecies *N. e. transversa*, *flavigaster* is both a vigorous biter in self-defense and a musker whose olfactory potency rivals that of skunks.

**Abundance**   Very common. Although sometimes less numerous than the broad-banded water snake in heavily wooded areas, the yellowbelly is the most abundant aquatic serpent in much of the eastern part of the state.

**Size**   Most adults are 2 to 3 feet long; the record is 53⅝ inches.

**Habitat**   A majority of rural wetland environments east of the blackland prairie, though yellowbelly water snakes are most numerous in swamps, the currentless water of oxbow river segments, bayous, and the marshy verges of floodplain lakes and ponds in far East Texas.

**Prey**   The young eat mainly tadpoles and aquatic insects; adults feed on fish, frogs, and other amphibians.

**Reproduction**   Live-bearing. Born in late summer after a 3½-month gestation period, most litters contain 10 to 30 young ranging from 9 to 11½ inches in length. Juveniles are saddled, laterally barred, and profusely speckled with dark brown over a creamy, sometimes pinkish ground color.

**Coloring/scale form**   Latin for "yellow," *flavi*, combined with *gaster*, Greek for "belly," describes the Texas race as the yellow-bellied western form of the eastern redbelly (*erythrogaster*) water snake. Slightly paler on its lower sides, *N. e. flavigaster*'s unpatterned dark back varies from the gray-backed animals found in East Texas and Louisiana to specimens intermediate in coloring between this race and the vertebrally pale-barred, laterally dark-blocked western subspecies, the blotched water snake. Marked only by the dark vertical sutures of the labial scales, the lips and chin are yellow, as is the belly. The dorsal scales are strongly keeled and arranged in 23 (usually) to 27 rows at midbody; the anal plate is divided.

**Similar snakes**   See blotched water snake (72).

**Behavior**   For the most part *Nerodia* (the new genus name for North American water snakes previously classified as *Natrix*) have not made a radical physical accommodation to aquatic life. Instead, they are able to take advantage of the rich food supply and protective murky milieu of ponds and bayous primarily by behavioral adaptations such as offsetting the heat-draining property of water—some 40 percent greater than that of air—by basking on logs, lily pads, and overhanging tree limbs. The annual congregations of toads that gather to breed in ditches and little temporary ponds draw yellowbellies a considerable distance away from their home lakes and rivers, however.

# Broad-banded Water Snake

*Nerodia fasciata confluens*

**Nonvenomous**   See Gulf salt marsh snake (75).

**Abundance**   Uncommon throughout much of its extensive East Texas range, N. f. confluens is sometimes locally abundant in the region's pine-hardwood swamps, as well as along the upper coast.

**Size**   Adult length averages 20 to 30 inches; the record is 45 inches.

**Habitat**   Permanent bodies of currentless water, particularly swampy, forest-bordered ponds and lakes; coastal prairie wetlands are also occupied.

**Prey**   Primarily cold-blooded vertebrates—fish, frogs, toads, and salamanders, as well as crayfish—seized on nightly forays along the banks and bottoms of creeks and ponds.

**Reproduction**   Live-bearing. Mating has been reported to occur on land during April, followed by 70 to 80 days of gestation, after which the largest females deliver litters of up to 50 young. Most broods, however, are closer in number to the 15 offspring—all between 8½ and 9 inches in length and about ⅓ ounce in weight—deposited on July 20 by a 32½-inch Smith County female.

**Coloring/scale form**   The dappled yellow belly is usually marked with large rectangular brown blotches; William Lamar of the University of Texas reports that some individuals have bright red ventral crossbars, however. Arranged in 21 to 25 rows, the dorsal scales are keeled, and the anal plate is divided.

**Similar snakes**   Water snakes' oval heads and snouts, round pupils, and lack of a sunken heat-sensing pit between eye and nostril set them off from the **western cottonmouth (97),** as does their proportionately longer, more gradually tapered tail. *Nerodia* typically swim and dive vigorously, moreover, while the cottonmouth's entire body is buoyantly suspended on the surface; if cornered, water snakes may strike, but they never gape motionless in threat as the cottonmouth sometimes does. The **Gulf salt marsh snake (75)** is N. f. confluens' longitudinally striped (1 pale vertebral and 2 pale gray lateral stripes separated by broad charcoal stripes), mostly brackish swamp and marine shore subspecies. Where both races occur together along the upper coast, intergrade individuals bearing various combinations of *clarkii*'s pale stripes and *confluens*' yellowish dorsolateral patches are not uncommon.

**Behavior**   Inclined to spend the day either basking (in cool weather) or hiding in bankside burrows or beneath vegetative debris, in the warmer months broad-banded water snakes are active mainly at night.

*AQUATIC SNAKES*

# Gulf Salt Marsh Snake

*Nerodia fasciata clarkii*

**Nonvenomous**   N. f. clarkii will bite only if molested.

**Abundance**   Formerly quite numerous; now less common due to widespread commercial development and pollution of the tidal wetlands.

**Size**   Adults average about 2½ feet in length; the record is 36 inches.

**Habitat**   Crayfish and fiddler crab burrows in the salt-grass-lined margins of the tidal mud flats are the primary microhabitat.

**Prey**   Small aquatic and marine life, probably frogs and crayfish primarily, but also reportedly killifish, mullet, and shrimp.

**Reproduction**   Live-bearing. The 9- to 10½-inch young resemble the adults except for their slightly bolder striping; they range in weight from ¼ to ⅓ ounce at birth.

**Coloring/scale form**   Between lateral rows of big, dark gray or maroon spots the midbelly bears a line of equally large yellowish-cream-colored ovals. The keeled dorsal scales are arranged in 21 to 25 rows at midbody, and the anal plate is divided.

**Similar snakes**   In Texas, no other water-living serpent has the Gulf salt marsh's strongly contrasting light and dark dorsolateral striping: **western cottonmouths (97)** have mostly unmarked (never longitudinally pale-lined) dark backs, vertically slit pupils, a pointed snout above an underslung lower jaw, and sunken facial pits. These aquatic vipers are more thick-girthed than water snakes, with a proportionately shorter tail. In the vine- and grass-covered coastal meadows, intergrade animals with the pale cheeks and lateral blotches of the subspecies **broad-banded water snake (74)** and the longitudinal light gray dorsolateral stripes of *clarkii* are not uncommon.

**Behavior**   The difficulties faced by marine reptiles with respect to fluid conservation are as severe as those confronting desert-dwellers, for not only is fresh water entirely absent from their environment but seawater, which is saltier than vertebrate body fluids, exerts a continual osmotic draw on their internal electrolyte balance. Scaly reptilian skin is a good barrier against the hydraulic imperative of liquids to equalize such discrepancies in mineral content, but because gastric and intestinal membranes are highly salt-permeable, if seawater is ingested, the gradient between it and the less salty surrounding tissues sucks fluid out of the organs and blood and into the stomach, eventually dehydrating any reptile not metabolically equipped, like the sea turtles, to rid itself of the extra salt. Among native ophidian species, only N. f. clarkii has managed to establish itself in an entirely saline niche along the Gulf Coast, apparently simply by swallowing nothing but its prey—whose body fluids are as dilute as its own.

# Florida Water Snake

## Nerodia fasciata pictiventris

**Nonvenomous**  Like other water snakes, *N. f. pictiventris* will bite only if molested.

**Abundance**  A breeding population has now established itself in southeastern Cameron County.

**Size**  In Florida, most adults are between 2 and 3½ feet in length.

**Habitat**  Texas' colony of *N. f. pictiventris* owes its existence to the live animal business operated in Brownsville by W. A. "Snake" King, which between 1907 and 1956 imported and sold thousands of wild creatures to zoos, circuses, and snake charmers. To provide food for more glamorous reptiles such as king cobras, hundreds of water snakes from everywhere in the Southeast were imported and held in ramshackle cages, many of which were torn open by the violent hurricane of September 5, 1933. In addition, rather than maintaining these nondescript "food snakes" during slack seasons, King's firm annually released large numbers in the local resacas and parks, from which, it was hoped, they might be recaptured when business improved; that not all were recovered is evident in the appearance here of newborn Florida water snakes over 25 years after their predecessors' introduction.

**Prey**  Presumably small aquatic life such as crayfish, salamanders, frogs, and fish.

**Reproduction**  Following a midwinter breeding season, the Florida population gives birth in late spring to as many as 57 distinctly dorsally crossbanded offspring, 7 to 10½ inches long.

**Coloring/scale form**  Named for its painted (*pictum* in Latin) belly, *N. f. pictiventris* is distinguished by the dark brown markings that border its yellowish belly scales and by the dark-edged reddish-brown crossbands (widest over the spine and sometimes outlined by white on the sides) that cross its gray-brown back; these bands are less evident on the tail. The grayish cheeks are paler than the dark crown and marked behind the eye with a short chocolate-colored stripe. There are 23 to 27 rows of keeled dorsal scales at midbody, and like that of all water snakes, the anal plate is divided.

**Similar snakes**  The only other *Nerodia* found in Cameron County is the **diamondback water snake (71)**. Dark lines form a rhomboid pattern on its gray-green to gray-brown back; dark vertical bars line its sides. It lacks both *N. f. pictiventris'* light-hued cheeks and dark postocular stripe and has a yellow belly distally flecked with dark spots.

**Behavior**  Presumably much like that of native Texas *Nerodia*.

*AQUATIC SNAKES*

# Green Water Snake

*Nerodia cyclopion cyclopion*

**Nonvenomous**  Like other large water snakes, if molested *N. cyclopion* will bite in its own defense.

**Abundance**  Spottily distributed near the upper Gulf Coast, as well as within the Sabine River drainage as far north as Marshall.

**Size**  Adults average 30 to 38 inches in length; the record is 51 inches.

**Habitat**  Along the coast green water snakes occur in open marshland vegetated with reeds and cattails and in wooded inland waterways.

**Prey**  An examination of 75 stomachs revealed frogs in 10, fish in 4, and a single large salamander in another; the young probably feed mostly on insects, tadpoles, and minnows.

**Reproduction**  Live-bearing. Litter size averages 15 to 25; the 9- to 11-inch newborns are more prominently spotted and dark-crossbarred than adults.

**Coloring/scale form**  *N. cyclopion*'s most definitive characteristic is the row of small subocular scales—found on no other aquatic snake—that rings the lower half of its eye, separating it from the upper labial scales (see illustration). The belly is also distinctive: yellowish white on the forequarters, then darkening over its posterior two thirds to gray, heavily infused with forward-arched yellowish-cream spots. Arranged in 27 to 29 rows at midbody, the dorsal scales are keeled; the anal plate is divided.

*Green water snake*

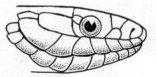

*Other water snakes*

***Similar snakes***  The angular head (sharply pointed snout, underslung chin, and slab-sided cheeks) of the **western cottonmouth (97)** contrasts with water snakes' more oval cephalic contours. Both the cottonmouth's indented dark facial pit between eye and nostril and its narrow vertical pupil—visible from several feet away—are sure identifying marks. The short little tail of the cottonmouth is also unlike the *Nerodia*'s long, tapered caudal configuration.

Both **yellowbelly (73)** and **blotched (72) water snakes** are distinguished by their largely unmarked yellow bellies and the direct contact of their upper labial scales with the lower margin of the eye. The blotched also has a pattern of short, dark-edged pale vertebral crossbars and dimly dark-blocked sides, and neither has more than 27 rows of dorsal scales. **Diamondback water snakes (71)** are patterned with a dorsal network of interlacing dark lines and, on their sides, vertical blackish-brown bars. They also lack subocular scales and have black-spotted yellow bellies.

***Behavior***  In Texas the green water snake seems to be almost exclusively nocturnal, for it is seldom observed either in the water or along the shore except by spotlighting after dark.

# Brazos Water Snake

*Nerodia harteri harteri*

**Nonvenomous**   Brazos water snakes will nip only if seized or molested.

**Abundance**   The only species of snake unique to Texas, *Nerodia harteri* is extremely restricted in range, with the nominative race being confined to the upper Brazos River drainage, where its adaptation to the faster-flowing portions of hill country waterways limits its habitat to a few hundred miles of river and tributary streams. Recent reservoir construction has inundated so much of this environment, however, that Brazos water snakes are now confined mainly to the as-yet-unflooded upstream sections of the 4 forks of the Brazos. Although Texas' most endangered serpent, where it occurs in these remaining channels *N. harteri* is often locally abundant.

**Size**   Adult length ranges from 16 to 32 inches, but few individuals measure more than 2 feet.

**Habitat**   *N. harteri* is found only on rocky portions of the upper Brazos River, where it typically hides under rocks along the banks or in shallow water.

**Prey**   The opportunity for predation on small fish as they become momentarily vulnerable in the riffles seems to be the primary factor determining this serpent's rapid-laced microhabitat.

**Reproduction**   Live-bearing. The parturition during September and early October of 4 females captured while gravid resulted in the birth of 7 to 22 young that measured 7¼ to 9 inches in length.

**Coloring/scale form**   The underside of the head and neck is cream to dark yellowish in color, but most of the belly is carrot orange; the ends of the ventral scales are spotted or darkened. Under the snout the posterior chin shields are separated by 2 rows of small scales; the keeled dorsal scales occur in 21 to 25 (usually 23) rows; and the anal plate is divided.

**Similar snakes**   The subspecies **Concho water snake (79)** has a less spotted belly and a single row of small scales between its posterior underchin shields. **Blotched water snakes (72)** have predominantly unmarked yellow bellies and gray-brown backs and sides patterned only with dark-edged pale vertebral crossbars and dimly defined dark lateral blocks.

**Behavior**   Since *N. harteri* is a generally diurnal and crepuscular forager, its exposed habitat requires it to spend long periods hiding from predators under rocks in the shallows. If discovered, its exceptionally fast getaway typically involves streaking diagonally downstream toward the opposite bank.

# Concho Water Snake

*Nerodia harteri paucimaculata*

Some 135 miles southwest of the Brazos River headwaters where *N. h. harteri* is found, the same sort of fast-flowing upper Colorado and Concho river riffles are home to Texas' other endemic, even more range- and habitat-restricted race of the Harter's water snake. Similar in most respects to the Brazos subspecies but not described until 20 years later, the Concho differs from *N. h. harteri* in having slightly paler brown dorsal markings and inconspicuous or absent ventral spots—hence its designation *paucimaculata,* or "fewer-spotted"—as well as but a single row of small scales separating the chin shields under its lower jaw. The throat is cream or pale yellow, the belly carrot-colored. Like the Brazos race, *paucimaculata* is a remarkably agile serpent: over distances of a few feet on land, it is as quick-moving as a racer or whipsnake, while no other indigenous serpent swims as rapidly.

The same habitat division between the still-water-living blotched water snake and the fast-water-living *N. h. paucimaculata* prevails on the Colorado-Concho watershed as exists in the Brazos drainage between the blotched and *N. h. harteri,* although the area may not retain these rare reptiles much longer. Since 1968 the Concho water snake's population has been decimated by the construction of Robert Lee Dam in Coke County, which by creating Spence Reservoir inundated over half of this animal's original habitat and left just 69 miles of Concho and Colorado riverbed in Tom Green, Concho, Coleman, and McCulloch counties along which it can live. Some 41 riffle sites (no individuals have been found more than 200 feet from such shallow rapids) along these rivers now contain almost the entire world population of 330 to 600 Concho water snakes, whose future is in considerable doubt, since Stacy Dam will flood and destroy at least 24.8 additional miles of their habitat. It will also so severely cut the downstream flow during dry weather that Concho water snakes may soon be confined to less than 22 miles of sparsely riffled streambed—a remnant environment probably both too small and too vulnerable to development (for these shallows are the best places to build low-water crossings and private ranch dams) to preserve the race from extinction.

*AQUATIC SNAKES*

# Graham's Crayfish Snake

*Regina grahamii*

**Nonvenomous**  Shy and nonaggressive, *Regina grahamii* is characterized by a generally calm temperament.

**Abundance**  Locally abundant in a few places, but throughout most of its wide Texas range, neither common nor generally dispersed.

**Size**  Small and slender, most adult *R. grahamii* measure only 18 to 30 inches in length; the maximum size is 47 inches.

**Habitat**  On the coastal plain, this animal inhabits sloughs, rice field irrigation ditches, and, in places where crayfish are common, muddy bottomland pastures. The aquifer-fed headwaters of rivers emanating from the Balcones Fault are also a minor habitat.

**Prey**  The stomachs of a number of Graham's have contained only freshly molted crayfish, although frogs and snails may also be taken.

**Reproduction**  Live-bearing. Late spring courtship and breeding reportedly occurs in the water at night, when several pheromone-drawn males may entwine themselves around a single female, forming a compact mass within which only a single copulation evidently occurs. More often, however, solitary breeding pairs float wrapped together, their tails hanging downward.

**Coloring/scale form**  The yellowish-cream belly's lateral border is delineated by a line of tiny, angular black spots, while a dim line of brown midventral dots is better defined on the posterior belly; the keeled dorsal scales are arranged in 19 rows at midbody, and the anal plate is divided.

**Similar snakes**  The **Gulf crayfish snake (81)** has a shiny, chocolate-colored back. A dim yellowish-tan stripe, split with a single black seam, occupies the first 3 scale rows above its pale belly, which is marked with a double row of rearward-arched dark brown crescents. The **Gulf salt marsh snake (75)** has a gray-striped back and sides, at least 21 rows of dorsal scales, and a dark-hued belly whose midline bears a row of big cream-colored ovals. **Blotched (72), yellowbelly (73), diamondback (71),** and **broad-banded (74)** water snakes lack both a horizontal color demarcation along their sides and dark midventral spots; their dorsal scales are arranged in 23 or more rows. The more thick-girthed **green water snake (77)** has a grayish, yellow-spotted posterior belly, a row of small scales between the lower edge of the eye and the upper labial scales, and 27 or more rows of dorsal scales.

**Behavior**  *R. grahamii* forages at night during the summer months but engages in more crepuscular activity in spring and fall; because of its exceptionally reclusive temperament, it is sometimes able to subsist in urban park ponds and drainage creeks where larger, more visible water snakes would soon be killed.

# Gulf Crayfish Snake

## Regina rigida sinicola

**Nonvenomous**   Like its relative the Graham's crayfish snake, this shy little reptile seldom bites, even if molested.

**Abundance**   Very uncommon.

**Size**   Adults average no more than 20 inches long; maximum recorded size is 31⅜ inches.

**Habitat**   R. rigida is both aquatic and semisubterranean, inhabiting the freshwater marshes, lakes, and inundated rice fields of the coastal plain, where it may burrow several inches into the earth beneath rotting stumps, logs, or planks at the water's edge.

**Prey**   Primarily crayfish, lesser sirens, small fish, frogs, and aquatic insects such as dragonfly nymphs.

**Reproduction**   Live-bearing; 11 newborns measured between 7¼ and 8½ inches in length.

**Coloring/scale form**   The back is shiny chocolate brown, occasionally very faintly striped with paler dorsolateral lines; a dim, yellowish-tan stripe along the first and second scale rows above the belly is split by a thin black seam. The lips are also yellowish, while the pale belly is marked by a double row of large, rearward-arched blackish crescents that form a single row beneath both chin and tail. The dorsal scales are keeled and arranged in 19 rows at midbody; the anal plate is divided.

**Similar snakes**   The more heavy-bodied **western cottonmouth (97)** has a much broader, flat-sided head with a sunken heat-sensing pit between eye and nostril and prominent eyes with vertically slit pupils. The yellowish lateral band of the **Graham's crayfish snake (80)** extends 3 scale rows above the belly, where it is separated from the grayish-brown back by a faintly serrated dark horizontal line. The Graham's belly also bears a single row of small midventral spots. **Green water snakes (77)** are uniformly dark-speckled above, with triangular yellow spots scattered over the gray posterior belly. There are 27 or more rows of dorsal scales, and a single row of little subocular scales separates the eye from the big scale plates along the upper lip. The **yellowbelly water snake (73)** also lacks a longitudinal color demarcation along its sides; it has 23 or more rows of dorsal scales and an unmarked belly.

**Behavior**   A strictly nocturnal forager active only between March and early November, R. r. sinicola is almost never observed because of its semisubterranean lifestyle.

*AQUATIC SNAKES*

# Western Mud Snake

*Farancia abacura reinwardtii*

**Nonvenomous**   Even when handled in the field, this big, docile serpent is generally unwilling to bite.

**Abundance**   Formerly fairly abundant in Wharton, Matagorda, Brazoria, and Galveston counties, *Farancia* is seldom seen at present, although its nocturnal, aquatic-burrowing behavior radically curtails its exposure to man.

**Size**   Although adults may reach over 6 feet, at hatching the young may be as small as 6¼ inches; most adults measure between 30 and 48 inches.

**Habitat**   Sluggish bodies of water with swampy margins and profuse aquatic vegetation are the preferred microhabitat; *Farancia abacura* has also been found under bankside logs and debris on hummocks in swampy bottomland forest.

**Prey**   A very species-specific predator, the western mud snake has a heavily muscled neck, jaws, and trunk adapted to overpowering large eels, three-toed amphiumas, and western lesser sirens.

**Reproduction**   Egg-bearing. Throughout the 8- to 12-week incubation period, the female sometimes remains coiled about her clutch within an elliptical bankside cavity (where her respiration could benefit the eggs by slightly raising the chamber's humidity); the eggs hatch in September and October.

**Coloring/scale form**   Rectangular extensions of the black dorsolateral pigment extend from either side onto the carmine-colored belly, where they describe a red-and-black checkerboard pattern that, beneath the tail, becomes a series of crossbands. The 19 rows of smooth dorsal scales are large and glossy; the anal plate is almost always divided.

**Similar snakes**   No other indigenous serpent bears the mud snake's distinctive color pattern. The **western cottonmouth (97)** is brownish or blackish gray rather than glossy blue-black above, has no reddish scallops along its lower sides, and is quite different in shape: the cottonmouth's trunk is much thicker than its narrow neck, while its angular, slab-cheeked head is characterized by an underslung chin, sunken facial pits and big, vertically slit-pupilled eyes.

**Behavior**   If captured, *F. a. reinwardtii* typically curls its tail tightly around one's wrist, pressing in its hardened, hornlike tip so firmly that it was once believed that this spur could deliver a mortal sting. *Farancia's* habit of lying in a circular coil was factored into the theory as well, giving rise to the legend of the horn or hoop snake that can grab its tail in its mouth to roll down a fleeing man and sting him to death with venom powerful enough to kill a tree.

# Texas Night Snake

### *Hypsiglena torquata jani*

**Mildly venomous**   Despite the jerky movements of its slightly triangular head, *Hypsiglena* never bites larger creatures, although its mildly toxic saliva has a paralytic effect on its diminutive reptile, insect, and annelid prey.

**Abundance**   A widespread little animal common (though seldom seen) in a variety of dry, terrestrial environments.

**Size**   Most adults are 10 to 14 inches in length; recorded to 20 inches.

**Habitat**   Microenvironment usually involves sandy or gravelly ground broken by rocky bluffs or overlain by flat stones and fallen branches; the South Texas thorn brush community is another major habitat.

**Prey**   Lizards, smaller snakes, worms, and insects have been reported.

**Reproduction**   Egg-bearing. Proportionately quite large—up to 1⅛ inches in length and ½ inch in diameter—night snake eggs have been found in Texas between early April and late June, usually in clutches of 4 to 6. Hidden beneath stones, decaying vegetation, or debris, they hatch after about 8 weeks.

**Coloring/scale form**   Big coppery eyes bulge from the flat cheeks and are slit by a vertical hairline pupil, while the dark brown blotches that mark the nape and sides of the neck are also definitive. The belly is white with a faint silvery sheen; except for the slightly ridged vertebral scales above the anal region of adult males, the 21 midbody rows of dorsal scales are smooth; the anal plate is divided.

**Similar snakes**   The **spotted night snake (84)** is a paler, western desert-living subspecies. One of the most common little suburban-environment reptiles, the **Texas brown snake (13)** lacks *Hypsiglena*'s 3 big, dark brown bars on the nape and sides of its neck; it has brown-blotched white cheeks (one blotch on the side of the neck, the other directly under the round-pupilled dark eye), 17 rows of keeled dorsal scales, and a bullet-shaped head little wider than its neck. Their tiny upturned snouts distinguish **western (48)** and **Mexican (49) hooknose snakes**—which also have but 17 rows of dorsal scales, round-pupilled dark eyes, and no very large brown nuchal blotches.

**Behavior**   Active principally after dark between April and late October, *H. t. jani* has the protruding eyes typical of many nocturnal reptiles, but it shares only with other toxic-saliva-bearing, rear-fanged colubrids and the pit vipers an elliptical pupil—whose vertical aperture protects the light-sensitive optic rods from bright light, yet after dark allows for more radical expansion than a circular pupil.

*MILDLY VENOMOUS REAR-FANGED SNAKES*

# Spotted Night Snake

*Hypsiglena torquata ochrorhyncha*

**Mildly venomous**   See Texas night snake (83).

**Abundance**   Common. Along the Rio Grande from Big Bend to the Quitman Mountains in southern Hudspeth County and northward almost to the Davis Mountains, the Texas night snake is replaced by its desert-living subspecies, *H. t. ochrorhyncha.*

**Size**   Similar to that of the Texas night snake (83).

**Habitat**   Both arid, sparsely vegetated flats and rocky mountain slopes to 5,000 feet in elevation.

**Prey**   Principally lizards, probably especially the banded geckos found under the same flat stones and sotol roots, as well as buried lizard eggs.

**Reproduction**   See Texas night snake (83).

**Coloring**   Like the pallid desert races of other widely distributed serpents, the spotted night snake is distinguished from the Texas form by its lighter brown vertebral blotches, its less evident lateral spotting, and its more whitish ground color.

**Similar snakes**   See Texas night snake (83).

**Behavior**   Probably identical to that of the Texas night snake (83).

# Black-striped Snake

*Coniophanes imperialis imperialis*

**Mildly venomous**  *Coniophanes'* weak salivary venom and rudimentarily grooved rear fangs allow it to subdue small vertebrate prey, but its calm temperament means that it is unlikely to bite human beings, in whom its saliva produces no serious or lasting effects.

**Abundance**  Known only from Cameron, Hidalgo, and Willacy counties, where the black-striped was numerous before World War II, although today it is uncommon because of the brush clearing that has devastated most of the Rio Grande Valley's wildlife habitat.

**Size**  Reported to 20 inches, adults usually measure between 12 and 18 inches in length.

**Habitat**  This secretive little serpent typically forages from late evening to early morning, avoiding daytime activity by burrowing into sandy soil or hiding under cacti, piles of fallen palm fronds, or logs. On the outskirts of Harlingen, black-striped snakes are edificial, turning up around buildings beneath long-discarded trash and construction debris.

**Prey**  Mostly small frogs and toads; probably also lizards, smaller snakes, and mice.

**Reproduction**  Egg-bearing. In Chiapas, Mexico, clutches have been found to number up to 10 eggs, which typically take only about 40 days to hatch into 6½-inch-long young.

**Coloring/scale form**  In contrast to the dark colors of its back and sides, *Coniophanes'* belly is orange to pink, its undertail bright red. There are 19 rows of smooth dorsal scales, and the anal plate is divided.

**Similar snakes**  No other serpent within its range is likely to be mistaken for the black-striped: **garter (23–29), ribbon (30–33),** and **patchnose (34–36) snakes** have pale yellow to orangish vertebral stripes and unmarked white bellies, with the garters and ribbons being further distinguished by their keeled dorsal scales and undivided anal plates.

**Behavior**  Like other red-undertailed serpents, *C. i. imperialis* characteristically inverts this part of its belly when harassed; with its foreparts lowered, it may then wave its elevated tail tip slowly back and forth in a threatening approximation of its about-to-bite head.

*MILDLY VENOMOUS REAR-FANGED SNAKES*

# Texas Lyre Snake

*Trimorphodon biscutatus vilkinsonii*

**Mildly venomous**   Vertically slit hairline pupils mark this as a mildly venomous serpent, whose posterior upper jaw carries a pair of slightly enlarged, grooved teeth. *T. b. vilkinsonii* poses no danger to humans, however, for unlike the vipers, it cannot inject muscle-pressurized venom. Instead, after a bite lyre snakes must advance their jaws far enough to engage the rear fangs, down whose lengthwise furrows the toxic saliva is squeezed by contractions of the jaw—a process far too time-consuming to affect large mammals able to break free immediately.

**Abundance**   Since a number of these extremely secretive animals turn up every summer in widely separated locales across the Trans-Pecos, lyre snakes seem to be broadly but very sparsely distributed throughout the northern Chihuahuan Desert. Nevertheless, since 1977 *T. b. vilkinsonii* has been protected from capture by the Texas Department of Parks and Wildlife.

**Size**   Adults are most often 24 to 36 inches in length; the record is 41 inches.

**Habitat**   Lyre snakes are nocturnal, mostly rock-crevice-dwelling desert residents found from Big Bend northwest to the Franklin Mountains of El Paso County, especially in jumbles of fallen boulders or along fissured bluffs.

**Prey**   Any small vertebrate prey, but primarily lizards: Dallas herpetologists observed one large *vilkinsonii* methodically searching a stony arroyo wall for the several species of lizards that had squeezed into its crevices for the night.

**Reproduction**   Egg-bearing. After a 77-day incubation period, one clutch hatched into very slender 8½-inch young that were marked exactly like the adults except for their more distinct dorsal patterning and the joining of the 3 dim spots on their crowns by a brownish line.

**Coloring/scale form**   *T. b. vilkinsonii*'s wiry neck supports an oval head notable for the big, slit-pupilled eyes associated with the development of a rudimentary venom system in several of Texas' rear-fanged snakes. The belly scales are buff on the posterior third, faintly yellowish or pinkish brown elsewhere. A little facial scale called a lorilabial is located between the loreal and upper labial scales; the dorsal scales are smooth, usually arranged in 23 rows at midbody, and the anal plate is divided.

***Similar snakes***   The **Trans-Pecos copperhead (100)** is a much more heavily proportioned, shorter-tailed serpent with broad mahogany dorsolateral bands. Its underslung lower jaw and pointed snout are distinctive, as is the dark heat-sensing pit between its eye and nostril. A pale, rearward-pointing V-shaped marking covers its cheek behind a projecting supraocular ridge, and its anal plate is undivided.

***Behavior***   Like a number of other arid-land-living serpents, the lyre snake makes its rare appearances in the open immediately after rainfall. The high percentage of adult males found at these times suggests that many of these animals are engaged in breeding forays, having been drawn out by the pheromonal scent stimuli intensified in the enhanced olfactory atmosphere associated with high humidity; females and young apparently seldom venture beyond the shelter of their residential canyons and rock piles.

*MILDLY VENOMOUS REAR-FANGED SNAKES*

# Northern Cat-eyed Snake

*Leptodeira septentrionalis
septentrionalis*

***Mildly venomous***   A pair of slightly enlarged rear teeth (along whose longitudinal grooves *L. s. septentrionalis'* mildly toxic saliva is channeled into the
wounds of its prey) enables this snake to immobilize small animals.

***Abundance***   Found only at the southern tip of the Rio Grande Valley, where
little of its native thorn brush and riparian woodland remains intact, this
subtropical creature is one of the rarest reptiles in Texas and has been protected from capture since 1977.

***Size***   Adults average 14 to 32 inches (females are slightly longer), with bodies
no thicker than a forefinger among even the largest individuals.

***Habitat***   The coastal Tamaulipan thorn thicket south of Falfurrias, in which
the principal microhabitat is likely to be dense vegetation bordering ponds
and watercourses, where this semiarboreal reptile's speed and agility provide
an effective means of flight from danger.

***Prey***   Primarily pond and tree frogs; given the feeding preferences of captives,
smaller snakes, minnows, and mice are probably also taken.

***Reproduction***   Egg-bearing. The clutches of Mexican females have been
found to vary in incubation time from 79 to 90 days; except for their bolder
dorsal patterning, the 9-inch-long young exactly resemble adults.

***Coloring/scale form***   The golden eyes slashed with fine-lined, vertically
elliptical pupils are shared with other rear-fanged, mild-venomed colubrids,
as well as with the pit vipers. The pale underchin and throat shade to light
orange at midbody and salmon beneath the tail, while the outer ends of
many of the belly scales, which have a slightly darkened posterior border, are
peppered with brown speckling. Arranged in 21 to 23 rows at midbody, the
dorsal scales are smooth, though some are pocked by tiny apical pits; the
anal plate is divided.

***Similar snakes***   All other boldly crossbanded serpents on the lower coastal
plain—the **coral (96), Mexican milk (90),** **Texas longnose (88),** and **Texas scarlet (95) snakes**—are girdled across their backs and sides with wide red
saddles or bands. These exclusively terrestrial, often burrowing animals are
characterized by small heads no wider than their necks and little dark eyes
with round pupils; all but the coral have an undivided anal plate.

***Behavior***   Extremely nocturnal. Both the cat-eyed and the lyre snake, a similarly salivary-venomed rear-fanged desert-dweller, have pursued a quite different predatory strategy than the pit vipers, developing toxins only as po-
tent as necessary to subdue their diminutive prey while, unlike the vipers,
maintaining the slender body shape that allows them to evade or hide from
predators more effectively.

# Texas Longnose Snake

*Rhinocheilus lecontei tessellatus*

**Nonvenomous**   *Rhinocheilus lecontei* does not bite, though if picked up suddenly, individuals may defecate and writhe in agitation.

**Abundance**   Sparsely distributed in the Panhandle, western Edwards Plateau, and Stockton Plateau grasslands; uncommon in Central Texas and the Trans-Pecos, but seasonally abundant in the thorn brush of South Texas, where it is often seen crossing roads on humid spring nights.

**Size**   Most adults are 16 to 30 inches long; the record is 41 inches.

**Habitat**   A burrower in the dry, gravelly soils of the western half of the state, the Texas longnose is most often found near the moisture of even seasonally flowing streams.

**Prey**   *Rhinocheilus* feeds primarily on lizards and small rodents, the latter constricted with a loop of the snake's body.

**Reproduction**   Egg-bearing. Clutches include 4 to 9 eggs deposited in an underground nest; after 2 to 2½ months the 6½- to 9½-inch young emerge, rather pallidly marked with pink dorsal saddles and whitish sides.

**Coloring/scale form**   The elongate rostral scale at the tip of the snout is the source of this creature's common and scientific names: *rhino* is Greek for "nose," *cheil* for "lip." The coloring of longnose snakes from different regions varies widely: the red and black dorsal pigment of most South Texas specimens is confined to squarish patches along the spine, while the black-speckled lower sides are otherwise yellowish; the belly is unmarked white. This color pattern prevails roughly as far northwest as Terrell County, to the west of which longnoses may have narrow, often hourglass-shaped black dorsolateral bands separating paler reddish areas scarcely evident on some black-speckled individuals; unlike South Texas animals, this population has large dark splotches on nearly every belly scale. The 23 midbody rows of dorsal scales are smooth, the anal plate is undivided, and as in no other nonvenomous serpent in Texas, the belly plates beneath the tail usually occur in a single row.

*RED-BANDED AND BLACK-BANDED SNAKES*

***Similar snakes*** Because an irregular scattering of pale scales borders the red vertebral saddles of many longnoses, bits of yellow and red coloring sometimes touch, possibly giving rise to confusion with the **Texas coral snake (96),** whose adjacent red and bold chrome-sulfur dorsolateral bands (2 or 3 scales in width) also encircle its belly. No pale area occupies the coral's lower sides, its stubby black nose is unlike the longnose's pointed, light-hued snout, its anal plate is undivided, and its undertail bears a double row of scales. The dorsal pattern of both the **milk snakes (89–92)** and the very rare **Texas scarlet snake (95)** involves comparatively narrow black crossbands, while their sides are devoid of yellow and black speckling; there is also a double row of scales under the tail in both species.

***Behavior*** If molested, the longnose, burying its head for safety in its coils, may wave its tail slowly about in a defensive posture thought to evoke among carnivores an image similar to that of the about-to-strike head and foreparts of the similarly crossbanded coral snake.

□ *Area of intergradation*

# Louisiana
# Milk
# Snake

*Lampropeltis triangulum amaura*

**Nonvenomous**   Because of their small size, Louisiana milk snakes seldom bite even if picked up, but like other members of the kingsnake family, occasional individuals may nip tenaciously.

**Abundance**   Widespread but rarely encountered because of their retiring semisubterranean habits, Louisiana milk snakes are sometimes found in late winter and early spring in crevices beneath the bark of pine stumps and logs. Later in the year, they live mostly as burrowers in sandy loam but may appear at the surface under flat rocks during rainy weather. Because of their bright colors, *L. triangulum* are avidly sought by reptile collectors, and while the impact of these people's demand on the natural population is infinitesimal compared with the inroads made by timbering and land clearing, every subspecies has been protected from capture in Texas since 1977.

**Size**   Recorded to 31 inches in length, although most adults are much smaller, averaging only 16 to 24 inches.

**Habitat**   Two primary habitats are the upper coastal plain, where *L. t. amaura* is found beneath the driftwood, planks, and littoral debris that mark the spring tide line of the Gulf barrier islands, and the East Texas pine and deciduous woodland, where it is found in riparian bottomland.

**Prey**   Much of the Louisiana milk snake's diet consists of the small serpents that, along with its secondary prey of skinks and spiny lizards, share its forest-floor microhabitat of leaf litter and humus.

**Reproduction**   Egg-bearing. See Central Plains milk snake (92).

**Coloring/scale form**   Because their ranges overlap so intricately, the 4 races of Texas' milk snake population are difficult to define with precision. The Louisiana form's black snout is often so mottled with white that the animal seems to have been nosing into flour; the posterior portion of its head is entirely black, followed by a pale collar, while broad red bands, ranging in number from 13 to 21 (average 16.2), are spaced along the trunk, pinched at the belly line by their narrower black borders. Between the black rings are light-hued bands whose color varies from pale yellow among the population living in the southern, coastal section of the range—and therefore subject to gene flow from the more yellowish-banded Mexican milk snake—to white in Northeast Texas. In both areas, the belly is predominantly pale along a central strip where the red and black pigment that encroaches onto the outer portion of the ventral scales seldom intrudes. Arranged in 21 midbody rows, the dorsal scales are smooth; the anal plate is undivided.

*RED-BANDED AND BLACK-BANDED SNAKES*

**Similar snakes**  Milk snakes' red and pale yellow or white dorsal hues never touch as they do on the **Texas coral snake (96),** which, unlike *L. triangulum,* has both wide black body bands (as broad as its red ones) and a divided anal plate. Also unlike the Louisiana milk, the coral snake has no whitish coloring: its back is banded with red, bright sulfur yellow, and black. The red dorsolateral bands of the **Mexican milk snake (90)** seldom narrow at the belly line and are generally darker along the spine; it has a blotchy, black midventral area and a mostly black snout. The **Central Plains milk snake (92)** generally has more profuse white flecks on its snout as well as a higher number—20 to 32 (average 25.6)—of narrower, more orangish dorsolateral rings. The **Texas longnose snake (88)** has roughly rectangular red and wide black vertebral saddles above black-speckled yellowish lower sides and a whitish belly. Its elongate snout is tan in color. There are 23 rows of dorsal scales, and under its tail, a single row of subcaudal scales (unlike the double row of the milk and other nonvenomous snakes) reaches from vent to tip. The **northern scarlet snake (94)** has a pointed red snout, an unmarked white belly, 19 midbody rows of dorsal scales, and red dorsolateral saddles that do not reach the belly line.

**Behavior**  Rather than mimicking the coral snake's bright pattern, milk snakes' striking dorsal hues may function primarily as camouflage. Because red looks gray at night, the only time *L. triangulum* forages at the surface, its crimson bands are inconspicuous to color-visioned snake predators such as owls, while, approximating dark shadows, its black crossbands break up the visual continuity of its serpentine shape. Its intervening pale dorsolateral rings further fragment its profile by resembling the light-dappled patchwork of the nighttime forest floor—an illusion enhanced by the milk snake's deliberate gait.

# Mexican Milk Snake

☐ *Area of intergradation*　　*Lampropeltis triangulum annulata*

**Nonvenomous**　Milk snakes will bite in self-defense, but usually only if roughly seized or molested.

**Abundance**　Seasonally not uncommon throughout the thorn thicket and irrigated farm country of South Texas, yet since *L. triangulum* are coveted by reptile hobbyists—many people keep them as living gems—all 4 native subspecies were given state protection in 1977.

**Size**　The largest of Texas' milk snakes, with adults averaging 20 to 32 inches in length; the record is 41½ inches.

**Habitat**　Both the semi-arid thorn brush of South Texas and the coastal barrier islands, where these animals are found under high-tide driftwood.

**Prey**　Like most *Lampropeltis,* milk snakes are powerful constrictors of other serpents, from rattlers to smaller members of their own species. Prey also includes lizards and small mammals.

**Reproduction**　Egg-bearing. See Central Plains milk snake (92).

**Coloring/scale form**　Only a few light anterior labial spots mark the otherwise black head; there are 14 to 20 (average 17.6) broad, dark red dorsolateral bands, often peppered along the spine with black. Their lower edges extend onto the otherwise pale belly scales, where they are cut off by blotchy strips of black pigment that occupy the midventral area. Arranged in 21 rows at midbody, the dorsal scales are small and glossy; the anal plate is undivided.

**Similar snakes**　While in milk snakes, red and yellow (or white) body bands touch only black bands, never each other, the more slender **Texas coral snake (96)** has adjacent red and yellow bands as well as much broader black dorsal bands (as wide as its red bands), which also encircle its belly. Its anal plate is divided. Where their ranges intersect, many *L. triangulum* show intermingled characteristics of both the Mexican and **Louisiana milk snake (89)** races, while phenotypically pure specimens of both forms are occasionally found deep within the territory of the other. See Louisiana milk snake (89). To the west, *L. t. annulata* merges with the **New Mexico milk snake (91),** which is distinguished by a greater average number of red dorsal bands (22.1), black dorsolateral rings much thinner than its comparatively broad white (rather than yellow) pale body bands, and a lighter-hued midventral area. The **Texas longnose snake (88)** is distinguished by squarish red vertebral saddles, numerous yellow or cream-colored scales scattered throughout its broad black dorsal crossbands, black-speckled yellowish lower sides, an extended brown or pinkish snout, and 23 rows of dorsal scales. The belly is whitish, with a single row of ventral scales beneath most of the tail. The

*RED-BANDED AND BLACK-BANDED SNAKES*

very rare **Texas scarlet snake (95)** has an orange or red snout, 19 midbody rows of dorsal scales, and red dorsal bands that fade to white 1 or 2 scale rows above its white belly.

*Behavior*  These brilliantly tricolored reptiles are anything but milky in appearance, their name apparently having stemmed from early attempts to explain their presence in dairy barns, where they were drawn in search of nestling mice. Since they were obviously too slow to catch agile adult rodents, it was thought that these little snakes subsisted by twining up the legs of milk cows after dark to suck their udders.

# New Mexico Milk Snake

*Lampropeltis triangulum celaenops*

**Nonvenomous**   *L. t. celaenops* will not bite unless handled.

**Abundance**   Throughout its wide range, this animal is almost never seen except at night during May and June, when it is typically observed moving rapidly across back-country ranch-to-market roads.

**Size**   Most adults are between 14 and 22 inches in length; the largest of 7 Texas specimens measured 25¼ inches.

**Habitat**   Rocky portions of the northern Chihuahuan Desert's lowland flats, as well as its evergreen mountain woodland.

**Prey**   Primarily smaller snakes, lizards located by scent in the crevices where they retreat for the night, and burrow- and rock-dwelling rodents.

**Reproduction**   Egg-bearing. See Central Plains milk snake (92).

**Coloring/scale form**   Arranged in 21 rows at midbody, *celaenops'* smooth dorsal scales have a bright, enamellike surface. The snout is black, flecked with white; the remainder of the head is black except for the whitish collar that marks its juncture with the neck. Dorsally, 17 to 25 (average 22.1) black-bordered carmine bands are separated by narrower white bands, to which a scattering of brown flecks may give a dirty gray appearance. The black body bands are often slightly wider over the posterior spine; the midbelly is largely without black pigment, and the anal plate is undivided.

**Similar snakes**   In the southeastern part of its range *L. t. celaenops* inhabits the same territory as the **Texas coral snake (96),** whose adjacent red and bright sulfur body bands touch; the milk snakes' red and white dorsolateral bands are separated by black rings. The coral's wide black body bands are as broad as its red ones, moreover, and all its bands encircle its trunk; its anal plate is divided. The **Central Plains milk snake (92)** is distinguished by its narrower and more numerous (20 to 32, average 25.6), often orangish dorsolateral bands; a bit of splotchy black pigment usually separates the lower edges of these bands along the belly's midline. The **Mexican milk snake (90)** is distinguished by its heavily black-pigmented midbelly, its pale yellow (rather than white) dorsolateral rings, and its fewer, wider red body bands (average 17.6). The **Texas longnose snake (88)** often has rectangular red and black vertebral saddles, as well as 23 rows of dorsal scales and a white belly with a single row of undertail scales, unlike the double row of milk snakes.

**Behavior**   In addition to their long winter dormancy, most western milk snakes undergo a similar hot-weather retirement during August and September, while during the rest of their April-to-November activity period they generally spend the daylight hours deep in subterranean crevices, where the humidity is higher and the temperature more constant than on the surface.

*RED-BANDED AND BLACK-BANDED SNAKES*

# Central Plains Milk Snake

*Lampropeltis triangulum gentilis*

***Nonvenomous***   Central Plains milk snakes will not bite unless handled.

***Abundance***   Rare, yet widely distributed; seldom found above ground.

***Size***   Reported to 3 feet in length, but adults average 16 to 24 inches.

***Habitat***   Brushy, rolling hillsides in short- or tallgrass prairie, especially where the soil is both broken with large rocks and loose enough for burrowing, moisture is present, and rodents and lizards are plentiful.

***Prey***   The young probably feed mainly on lizards, skinks, and miniature serpents such as blind snakes and *Tantilla*, as well as on earthworms and insects; adults also prey on small rodents and other snakes nearly as large as themselves, both of which are subdued by constriction.

***Reproduction***   Egg-bearing. After springtime breeding and gestation, followed by 65 to 80 days' incubation, the clutches of up to ten 1¼-by-⅝-inch adhesive-shelled eggs hatch into 7½- to 11-inch young.

***Coloring/scale form***   Variable: northern individuals have less vivid orange, black, and yellowish-gray dorsolateral bands than those from the southwestern Panhandle and North Central Texas, which intergrade with more colorful southern races. Among true *gentilis* the dull reddish-orange dorsolateral bands are narrower and more numerous (20 to 40, average 25.6) than those of other milk snakes, and are bordered by narrow black rings that may almost entirely encircle the russet bands low on the sides and belly (only intermittently do the yellowish-gray dorsolateral rings cross the belly). A few black scales also darken the orangish dorsolateral bands over the posterior spine. The head has a white-mottled snout and forehead, the 21 midbody rows of dorsal scales are smooth and glossy, and the anal plate is undivided.

***Similar snakes***   The Central Plains milk intergrades with the **Louisiana milk snake (89)** almost as far south as Fort Worth, where the latter is distinguished by its fewer, wider, and brighter red dorsolateral bands (an average of only 16.2) as well as by its pale midventral area. The **New Mexico milk snake (91)** also has fewer, wider, and redder body bands (averaging 22.1 in number), whitish pale body bands, and a light-hued midbelly. The **Texas longnose snake (88)** has black-speckled yellowish lower sides as well as often squarish red and black dorsal saddles; its unmarked white belly, unlike those of other nonvenomous snakes, generally has but a single row of subcaudal scales.

***Behavior***   Perhaps because so much of its macrohabitat consists of exposed prairie, *L. t. gentilis* seldom risks basking in the open and, to elevate its body temperature during cool spring weather, more often seeks warmth under sun-heated flat rocks.

# Gray-banded Kingsnake

*Lampropeltis alterna*

**Nonvenomous**   This gentle animal seldom nips even when picked up in the field.

**Abundance**   Controversial. Gray-banded kingsnakes are almost never seen except at night, crossing Trans-Pecos ranch roads east of El Paso and south of Fort Stockton. (Most are adult males engaged in cross-country courtship forays.) Yet in places this animal is not uncommon, especially immediately after rainfall, during April, May, and June. In 1980 it was denied federal designation as a threatened species, but it is still protected from capture in Texas by state law because, due to their often brilliant colors, gray-banded kings are among the most desirable serpents to reptile buffs. So few highways bisect *L. alterna*'s habitat, however, that collectors have access to only the tiny percentage of the population that lives near public roads, and the minuscule loss of those taken in this way is ecologically insignificant.

**Size**   As adults gray-banded kings average around 32 inches in length.

**Habitat**   Primarily rocky limestone ridges within the acacia-lechuguilla-sotol succulent desert of Val Verde, Terrell, and Brewster counties.

**Prey**   Probably mostly cornered or nestling rodents and sleeping lizards located by scent after dark. *L. alterna* is also the only non-snake-eating member of the kingsnake family.

**Reproduction**   Egg-bearing. Although no reproductive behavior has been observed in the wild, captive courtship often begins with dominance competition in which 2 adult males attempt to force each other to the ground; if a female is present, the more assertive combatant will then copulate with her. The clutches of 3 to 13 eggs, 1¼ to 1⅝ inches in length, are laid between late May and July, hatching into 9- to 12-inch-long young after approximately 9 weeks.

**Coloring/scale form**   Every gray-banded king is unique in coloring, although 2 basic color phases are typical: in the lower Pecos and Devil's river drainages most individuals have orange saddles separated from wide gray bands by narrower, sometimes thinly white-edged black rings; among more northerly specimens thin black bands—sometimes narrowly split with red— separate darker gray bands. The belly is pale gray, irregularly blotched with black; the 25 midbody rows of dorsal scales are smooth and glossy, and the anal plate is undivided.

*RED-BANDED AND BLACK-BANDED SNAKES*

***Similar snakes*** The proportionately more slender **Texas coral snake (96)** has adjacent yellow and red body bands that (along with its very wide black bands) encircle both its back and its belly. Its tiny black head is marked only with a prominent chrome-yellow sash behind the eye, and its anal plate is divided. The **New Mexico milk snake (91)** has 21 rows of dorsal scales and broad red dorsolateral bands bordered by thin black rings; each pair of red and black bands is separated by a prominent dirty white band. The **Texas longnose snake (88)** has dark-speckled yellowish lower sides, a long brownish snout, and no wide gray dorsolateral bands; unlike that of *Lampropeltis*, its white belly has but a single row of scales beneath most of the tail.

***Behavior*** Only in 1975 was it discovered that in order to breed, captive gray-banded kings need an enforced winter dormancy of 2 to 4 months in an unheated room. Large outside windows enable these animals to pick up the seasonal rhythm of the gradually lengthening daylight of early spring, while other sophisticated husbandry includes building false floors into their cages with entrance holes leading to an "underground" space filled with loose vermiculite where they can burrow during the day, then emerge onto the surface at night to feed. The result is that hundreds of young *alterna* are now bred in captivity every year.

# Northern Scarlet Snake

*Cemophora coccinea copei*

**Nonvenomous**  Northern scarlet snakes seldom bite, even when picked up in the wild.

**Abundance**  Locally common: especially during May and June, C. c. copei is among the most prevalent nocturnal serpents seen on many East Texas back roads.

**Size**  Most adults measure 14 to 20 inches in length.

**Habitat**  Primarily an inhabitant of the sandy or loamy soil of pine, hardwood, and mixed forest environments, the northern scarlet also invades a variety of adjacent open, also soft-soiled terrain, including the borders of swamps, stream banks, and agricultural fields.

**Prey**  Reptile eggs are evidently the preferred food, and to puncture the leathery shells of those too large to be swallowed whole, C. c. copei has evolved enlarged teeth in the rear of its upper jaw.

**Reproduction**  Egg-bearing. The 3 to 8 eggs, 1 to 1⅜ inches in length, are laid during late June or July; the young, which are colored differently from the adults (see Coloring/Scale Form), are 5½ to 6 inches at hatching.

**Coloring/scale form**  Because the scarlet snake's appearance changes radically with age, hatchlings, subadults, and very old individuals look almost like different species. At hatching, pink dorsal saddles extend only a short way down the sides, while black flecks almost touch the ventral scales below each saddle. As the animal grows older, these flecks gradually become the dark lower borders of the steadily reddening dorsal blotches, which eventually develop a broad black lateral edging. Among very old scarlet snakes, the colors dull, with the once-carmine saddles fading to dark reddish brown and the white spaces between them tarnishing with tan or gray. The unmarked belly is white, the smooth dorsal scales are arranged in 19 rows at midbody, and the anal plate is undivided.

**Similar snakes**  The **Texas coral snake (96)** has red and bright yellow bands that border one another and (along with its very wide black bands) extend unbroken across its belly. Unlike the scarlet snake's elongate orangish nose, the coral's stubby snout is jet black, while its anal plate is divided. The **Louisiana milk snake (89)** usually has a white-flecked black nose, dorsolateral bands that extend onto its red, white, and black ventral scales, and 21 rows of dorsal scales.

**Behavior**  This reptile seldom appears in the open except on late spring and early summer nights, for it is almost entirely subterranean in the daytime. During building excavation and road construction scarlet snakes have been uncovered as much as 6 feet below the surface.

*RED-BANDED AND BLACK-BANDED SNAKES*

# Texas Scarlet Snake

*Cemophora coccinea lineri*

**Nonvenomous**   *C. c. lineri* is unlikely to bite if carefully handled.

**Abundance**   Very rare.

**Size**   Texas scarlet snakes grow to a length of at least 26 inches.

**Habitat**   Almost the only habitat in which this animal has been observed is sand-floored thicket immediately adjacent to the Gulf Coast.

**Prey**   Although a sometime constrictor—small lizards and snakes are probably taken occasionally—*C. c. lineri* seems to feed largely on reptile eggs, which it punctures with the slightly enlarged teeth located in the rear of its upper jaw.

**Reproduction**   Egg-bearing. Reproduction is probably similar to that of its northern subspecies, *C. c. copei* (94).

**Coloring/scale form**   Both races of scarlet snake have a grayish-white dorsolateral ground color, with 17 to 24 heavily black-bordered, carmine to coral-red saddles spaced along the back. In the Texas scarlet, however, the black border of these saddles does not join across their lower edges as it does in the northern subspecies. Smooth and glossy, *C. c. lineri*'s dorsal scales are arranged in 19 rows at midbody, its belly is whitish, and its anal plate is undivided.

**Similar snakes**   The **Texas coral snake (96)** has a round little black nose unlike the scarlet's long orangish snout, a divided anal plate, and red and bright yellow body bands that both border each other and (along with the very wide black body bands) encircle its belly as well as its back. The **Mexican milk snake (90)** has a blunt black nose, a red, white, and black underside, and 21 midbody rows of dorsal scales, while the **Texas longnose snake (88)** usually has rectangular black dorsolateral saddles, black-speckled yellowish lower sides, 23 rows of dorsal scales, and a whitish belly with a single row of undertail scales (unlike the double row of every other harmless snake in the state).

**Behavior**   *C. c. lineri*'s activity cycle is probably similar to that of its northern subspecies, although few field observations have been made; captives ordinarily remain buried in the loose sand of their cage bottoms during the day, emerging to prowl about the surface only at night.

*ELAPIDAE*

# Texas Coral Snake

*Micrurus fulvius tenere*

**Venomous**  The venom is more virulent than that of any other North American reptile, at least 8 times as lethal as that of the western diamondback rattler and approxiately equal in potency to the toxins of most cobras. Since its entire volume is made up of neurotoxically destructive peptides, the lethal dosage for a healthy human adult is estimated to be as little as 5 to 10 milligrams. Although immediate pain usually accompanies a bite by one of these animals, central nervous system depression may not manifest its first symptoms for several hours. Therefore, in cases of definite envenomation antivenin should probably not be withheld until the onset of difficulties, because once symptoms appear it has proven difficult to prevent further decline.

   Yet very few people are harmed by coral snakes—only about 1 percent of snake venom poisonings involve *M. fulvius*, while many coral snake bites fail to result in envenomation. At less than ⅛ inch in length, their tiny, rigid fangs—grooved pegs rather than the hollow hypodermic tubes of the pit vipers—are too short to penetrate shoe leather or clothing. Where they can make contact, corals have no difficulty biting a large adversary, however, and can easily puncture a nipped-out pinch of skin almost anywhere on the human body, while in confined areas they can both crawl and snap sideways with alacrity. But if unmolested these little reptiles are typically so nonaggressive toward people that virtually everyone bitten by one has first touched or handled it.

**Abundance**  Very common. Since coral snakes are not at all averse to human habitation, they are far more likely to be encountered in suburban areas than their seldom-seen nocturnal look-alikes, the milk snakes, which prefer more natural terrain.

**Size**  Texas coral snakes are larger than most people expect: 74 adult females averaged 26½ inches in length, 93 males just over 24 inches. The record is a 47¾-inch Brazoria County specimen.

**Habitat**  Dry terrestrial milieus, especially the eastern pine forest, central oak-juniper brakes, and South Texas thorn brush. Either rock-crevice cover or thick plant litter is important, both as a hiding place and as habitat for the semisubterranean serpents on which coral snakes prey.

**Prey**  Chiefly snakes, although skinks and other lizards are occasionally taken.

**Reproduction**   "No other North American snake has been reported to breed from late summer–early autumn to late spring–early summer, then lay its eggs in midsummer," writes Hugh Quinn (Copeia 1979:453–63). The 3 to 5 white, slightly sausage-shaped eggs—about 1⅜ inches in length and ⅜ inch in diameter—are laid during June and July, hatching 2 months later into 6½- to 7½-inch young.

**Coloring/scale form**   The only black-, red-, and yellow-banded serpent in Texas whose red and yellow bands touch; if "red against yellow, kill a fellow" is usually too extreme a prognosis, it's still the best way to identify a coral snake quickly. Lined with 15 midbody rows of smooth dorsal scales, the trunk is patterned by 12 to 16 equally broad red and black bands separated by much narrower bright yellow rings. No red bands occur either posterior to the vent or forward of the nape: both head and tail are ringed only with black and yellow. All the dorsal bands continue uninterrupted across the belly, whose undertail has a double row of scales similar to that of most nonvenomous snakes; the anal plate is divided.

**Similar snakes**   Both the more heavily proportioned **milk snakes (89–92)** and the **scarlet snakes (94–95)** superficially resemble *Micrurus fulvius*, except that nowhere do their red and pale yellow or white body bands touch, being separated by narrow black rings: "red against black, venom lack." Only *M. fulvius* has black body bands as wide as its red ones, while milk and scarlet snakes' dorsolateral crossbands do not continue uninterrupted across their bellies and their red bands occur all the way to the tail tip. Milk snakes have 21 rows of dorsal scales, scarlets 19; the latter also have elongate orangish snouts and unmarked white bellies. On the nonvenomous **Texas longnose snake (88)** a *few* red and creamy yellow scales may touch, but only in the speckled edging of the red dorsal saddles. The belly is white, sometimes with speckled edges, the undertail scales occur in a single row, the protruding snout (unlike the coral's stubby black nose) is usually light brown, and the rear of the skull is devoid of a wide yellow band.

**Behavior**   To what degree the coral's bold patterning functions as a warning signal has long been an area of controversy, since its bright dorsolateral hues are probably inconspicuous to the largely color-blind mammals that feed on small terrestrial serpents. See Louisiana milk snake (89). Yet the bold contrast of the coral's body bands, combined with its distinctive posture and movement, do seem to function as a deterrent to predators: in order to capitalize on the threat of its venom while risking only its most expendable extremity to attack, *Micrurus fulvius* may tuck its foreparts under its trunk while waving its yellow-and-black-banded tail tip in imitation of its similarly patterned threatening head.

*VIPERIDAE*

# Western Cottonmouth

*Agkistrodon piscivorus leucostoma*

**Venomous**   Despite the cottonmouth's formidable reputation, comparatively few people are bitten: only about 7 percent of Texas' snakebites involve *A. piscivorus*, while throughout the United States the mortality rate is less than one person per year. Though rarely fatal, *A. piscivorus* envenomation is often serious in terms of tissue death, for while its toxins have far less lethal potency than those of the western diamondback rattlesnake, their destructiveness toward blood cells and plasma is nearly 9 percent greater than those of the diamondback.

**Abundance**   Very abundant in some areas, especially on the coastal plain.

**Size**   The record western cottonmouth, taken on the Neches River by George O. Miller, is just over 5 feet in length. Most are much smaller, however: of 306 individuals, only a few males were longer than 3 feet, while the majority of adults measured between 20 and 30 inches.

**Habitat**   Woodland or grassland, most often within a quarter-mile of permanent water. (Cottonmouths favor semiaquatic habitats primarily because of the more plentiful prey and better cover available there, but they do quite well in entirely dry environments.) Because cottonmouth populations tend to vary in density throughout the range, large areas of apparently good habitat are entirely devoid of these reptiles.

**Prey**   Frogs are this viper's most frequent prey in most locales, but *A. piscivorus* is an indiscriminate feeder whose diet alters with the availability of different vertebrate prey, including fish, mammals as large as muskrats and young cottontails, water birds, and sizable water snakes, as well as copperheads and smaller cottonmouths.

**Reproduction**   Live-bearing. The 3 to 12 young (the average is about 5, for the 7½- to 11-inch newborns are so thick that gravid females carry relatively few offspring) are born during August, September, and early October. Juveniles are somewhat paler and much more distinctly patterned with chocolate and light grayish brown than the adults, while their tail tips are yellowish or light greenish gray.

*Coloring/scale form*  Sometimes displayed in open-jawed threat, the creamy interior of the mouth is the source not only of this heavy-bodied reptile's common name but of its scientific denomination as well, for *Agkis* is a mistranslation of *ancil*, meaning "forward"; *odon* refers to its fangs; and *piscivorus* means "fish-eating." *Leuco* is "white" and *stoma* is "mouth," so the entire appellation accurately describes a forward-fanged, white-mouthed, fish-eating serpent. In daylight the pupils of the large, grayish eyes are vertical black slits easily visible from a safe distance; at night in the beam of a flashlight they appear slightly more rounded for the few moments it takes them to close against the glare. Definitive but less evident are the dark orifice of the heat-sensing pit located between the eye and nostril and the pronounced taper from the cottonmouth's thick posterior trunk to the attenuated little tail that, especially among females, sometimes seems out of proportion with the rest of the snake.

The keeled dorsal scales are arranged in 25 rows at midbody, while the subcaudal scales occur in a unique pattern by which even from their shed skins *Agkistrodon* can be identified: a single row of belly-wide scales covers the undertail behind the undivided anal plate.

*Similar snakes*  Primarily because they share comparatively thick trunks, dark, dimly patterned backs and sides, and the same aquatic habitat, adult cottonmouths closely resemble big **blotched (72), yellowbelly (73), and diamondback (71) water snakes**. Water snakes lack heat-sensing facial pits, however, and have rounded (though triangular-shaped when seen from above) heads and snouts, round pupils, a divided anal plate, and a double row of scales under the tail from vent to tip. Cottonmouths also behave differently from water snakes. They are less agile and sometimes hold their ground and gape openmouthed in threat; water snakes neither gape nor vibrate their tails in agitation like the cottonmouth. *A. piscivorus* also swims in a leisurely fashion, its entire body floating buoyantly with its head lifted slightly above the surface and angled forward, while water snakes swim by wriggling rapidly along, their bodies drooping into the water if they stop.

*Behavior*  The most widespread story about cottonmouths concerns the water-skier purportedly killed by a flurry of bites after tumbling into a nest of these reptiles: for years assorted versions of this fictitious event have circulated in boating circles, but no hospital or news agency in Texas has ever recorded the death of a water-skier from multiple *A. piscivorus* envenomation. Although some members of this species show little fear of humans, most retreat before larger mammals, with few pausing to threaten an intruder with open jaws if they have a way to escape. This gape is actually mostly a rather passive defensive gesture, and since such wide-jawed cottonmouths often fail to strike even when prodded with a boot, *A. piscivorus* is considerably less dangerous than similar-sized rattlesnakes, among whom such forbearance would be unlikely.

*MOCCASINS*

# Southern Copperhead

*Agkistrodon contortrix contortrix*

**Venomous**   Within its East Texas range the southern copperhead is responsible for the majority of venom poisonings, mostly due to its prevalence in wooded suburban neighborhoods. Yet records of the Antivenin Institute of America show that regardless of the kind (or lack) of treatment, throughout the country not a single death resulted from 308 copperhead bites over a 10-year period. This is largely because the digestive enzymes that precipitate local tissue death are only about half as destructive in the copperhead's toxins as in an equal quantity of western diamondback venom, although poisoning by *A. contortrix* occasionally causes the loss of a limb or digit, and could be fatal to a small child.

**Abundance**   In woodlands throughout the eastern third of the state, *A. c. contortrix* is generally the most numerous venomous snake; it is most often seen between March and October.

**Size**   Most adults measure 18 to 30 inches; probably none in Texas exceeds 38 inches.

**Habitat**   *A. c. contortrix* is almost always found in at least partially tree-shaded areas where leaves, pine needles, logs, and branches offer terrestrial shelter; southern copperheads seem to be more common in mixed pasture and woodland, however, than in longleaf pine forest.

**Prey**   Copperheads generally take whatever prey is most available at any time of year, though white-footed and harvest mice are probably *A. c. contortrix*'s principal food species.

**Reproduction**   Live-bearing. See broad-banded copperhead (99).

**Coloring/scale form**   This comparatively light-hued eastern subspecies' most distinctive characteristic is the 13 to 20 pale-centered brownish bands that, though quite broad at the belly line, are cinched or contorted—thus the Latin *contortrix*—into an hourglass configuration over the spine. On the wedge-shaped light tan crown, a pair of dark spots generally dot the rear of the skull. Prominent supraocular plates are part of a sharply angled intersection between the crown and the flat, undercut cheeks. Behind the big slit-pupilled, coppery eyes, the cheeks are marked with a rearward-pointing pale V whose upper border is defined by a dark line leading from the eye to the rear of the jaw; just below and behind the nostril is the dark heat-sensor pit. Arranged in 23 to 25 rows at midbody, the dorsal scales are weakly keeled; the anal plate is undivided.

**Similar snakes** The typical **broad-banded copperhead (99)** can be distinguished from the southern race found along the boundaries of its range by its more mottled belly, the absence of well-defined dark borders on its reddish-tan dorsolateral bands, and the almost equal width of these bands at the belly line and along the spine. The nonvenomous serpent most commonly mistaken for the southern copperhead is the **eastern hognose snake (44)**, especially in its coppery color phases, for both similarly patterned, heavy-bodied serpents occur in the same wooded suburban neighborhoods, and both show little fear of people. The hognose's slightly raised forehead, round-pupilled little dark brown eyes, comparatively thick neck, and prominently upturned snout are distinctive, however, as is its divided anal plate and the double row of scales beneath its tail (copperheads have a single row).

As a juvenile, the **western cottonmouth (97)** superficially resembles the young southern copperhead but is dark gray-brown instead of reddish tan. Newborn *A. p. leucostoma* also have a wide, pale-outlined *dark* band across their cheeks, and are seldom found away from water in the copperhead's woodland habitat.

**Behavior** Unlike rattlesnakes, which tend to move out of an area at the first sign of extensive urbanization, copperheads have adapted well to the presence of man and often occur in wooded suburbs. Although normally entirely terrestrial, after floods southern copperheads have been seen on the boughs of sloping cottonwoods, where they usually lie quietly, draped along the larger limbs.

# Broad-banded Copperhead

*Agkistrodon contortrix laticinctus*

**Venomous**   See southern copperhead (98).

**Abundance**   Often very common in areas of ideal habitat, typically light to moderate ground cover under a leafy sylvan canopy—including wooded suburban residential areas. Prime deciduous forest-meadow may support as many as 7 animals per acre.

**Size**   Similar to that of the southern copperhead (98).

**Habitat**   Almost everywhere in their range broad-banded copperheads occur most frequently in mesic upland woods on a thick carpet of oak leaves—against which they are particularly well camouflaged—although this reptile is also quite abundant in bottomland on the eastern Edwards Plateau.

**Prey**   Primarily rodents (especially deer and harvest mice), nestling ground birds, spiny lizards, and large insects, the latter accounting for up to 20 percent of the total volume of prey.

**Reproduction**   Live-bearing. Copulation takes place during both late fall and spring, with spermatozoa from the autumn pairings remaining viable throughout the female's winter retirement to fertilize the first ova she produces after vernal emergence. Born during the latter part of July and all of August and September, the 4 to 8 neonates are 7½ to 10 inches long and generally have paler dorsal pigmentation than their parent.

**Coloring/scale form**   To accommodate the big venom glands located behind the corners of the mouth, the rear of the skull broadens to more than 3 times the width of the narrow neck, while ahead of the eyes and slightly below the level of the nostrils lie the sunken heat-sensing pits. The pale belly is indistinctly mottled with reddish brown. Arranged in 23 (occasionally 25) rows at midbody, the dorsal scales are weakly keeled, and under the tail the belly scales are arranged in a single row behind the vent; the anal plate is undivided.

**Similar snakes** The hourglass-shaped, chocolate-bordered dorsolateral bands of the **southern copperhead (98)** generally narrow to solid brown bars across its spine; its cream- to buff-ground-colored belly is only distally splotched with large brown ovals. The **Trans-Pecos copperhead (100)** is distinguished by its more heavily pigmented belly, which ranges from dark chestnut to near-black, interrupted by pale lateral intrusions. Among *pictigaster* from far West Texas, the dorsolateral crossbands often bear a pale central aura around a dark mahogany spot just above the belly line, as well as a whitish bordering wash, while the area between the reddish bands may be almost white. On the average, there are more undertail scales (52 to 59 to the broad-banded's 37 to 54); there may also be fewer dorsal scale rows (21 to 25). Seen from above, **hognose snakes (44–47)** have a proportionately thicker neck than vipers, beady dark eyes with round pupils, a bulbous forehead, and a markedly upturned snout; they also lack the broad-banded's grayish tail tip and have a divided anal plate and a single row of undertail scales. Newborn *A. c. laticinctus* are dorsally patterned somewhat like the darker but similar-shaped young **western cottonmouth (97),** although their cheeks have a rearward-facing pale V in place of the blackish sides of the cottonmouth's head. Both species are often abundant in riverbottom woodland, but the cottonmouth, unlike the copperhead, seeks shelter in water.

**Behavior** *Agkistrodon contortrix*'s activity pattern varies considerably throughout the year. Beginning with springtime emergence from winter denning, these small animals seek their optimal temperature of 78 to 80 degrees Fahrenheit by basking during midday and hiding beneath woodland debris in the morning and evening. As midday temperatures climb beyond this level, copperheads grow more crepuscular, except on overcast days or when soil and vegetation are damp; in the hottest weather of midsummer, they hunt mostly at night.

# Trans-Pecos Copperhead

*Agkistrodon contortrix pictigaster*

***Venomous*** The venom of *A. c. pictigaster* has been found to be some 11 percent less lethal to mice than even the relatively mild toxins of the eastern copperheads. See southern copperhead (98).

***Abundance*** Especially in places such as the broken, canyon-laced region north of Langtry in Val Verde and Crockett counties, Trans-Pecos copperheads are among the most commonly seen nocturnal snakes, while they are also not uncommon in the rolling Terrell County plains, which are almost entirely devoid of canyons, rocky hiding places, and creeks.

***Size*** Most adults are 18 to 26 inches long; the record is 32⅞ inches.

***Habitat*** Although in places a shrub-desert-living serpent, the Trans-Pecos copperhead is found more often in the vicinity of the scattered permanent springs and streams remaining from the verdant West Texas of late Pleistocene times.

***Prey*** Presumably much the same as that of broad-banded (99) and southern (98) copperheads.

***Reproduction*** Live-bearing. See broad-banded copperhead (99).

***Coloring/scale form*** *A. c. pictigaster*'s dark dorsal bands vary from sandy brown to cinnamon-bay to dark seal brown, usually with a pale area at the base of each band (juveniles are palest). The heavily mottled ventral pigmentation, typically mahogany to black interrupted with pale lateral intrusions, is both unique to this subspecies and the source of its scientific name: *picti* means "painted" and *gaster* is "stomach." The tail is grayish brown above, with thin white crossbands, while a single line of undertail scales follows the vent. The 21 to (usually) 23 midbody rows of dorsal scales are weakly keeled; the anal plate is undivided.

***Similar snakes*** The **broad-banded copperhead (99)** is distinguished from the Trans-Pecos race by its less heavily mottled belly and its lower average number of subcaudal scales (52 to 59 in *pictigaster,* 37 to 54 in *laticinctus*). In the field such distinctions are largely arbitrary, however, since across a roughly east-west sequence of variation Texas' 3 copperhead subspecies only gradually diverge into their respective pure forms.

***Behavior*** *A. c. pictigaster*'s survival in a region now considerably drier than at any time during its prior occupation is largely due to the superiority of the pit vipers' predatory adaptations. Excellent night vision, heat-sensing facial pits, sophisticated venom, and delicately controllable erectile fangs—requiring only the minimal energy expenditure of a 5-inch striking jab—enable it to kill a high percentage of the small prey animals that come within range.

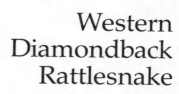

# Western Diamondback Rattlesnake

### *Crotalus atrox*

***Venomous*** The largest, most widespread, and statistically most dangerous (*atrox* is Latin for "frightful" or "grim") serpent in the state. Nearly all the most serious cases of snakebite treated in Texas hospitals every year are inflicted by *Crotalus atrox*, whose venom contains roughly 17 percent neurotoxically active peptide components, 30 percent tissue-digestive proteases, and 53 percent blood-targeted toxic enzymes. Affectively, western diamondback envenomation is characterized by immediate severe pain, accompanied by swelling, weakness, sweating and chills, faintness or dizziness, elevation or depression of pulse rate, nausea and vomiting, and swelling of the regional lymph nodes.

Yet few people die from diamondback bites. Widely available hospital care at facilities accustomed to combating hypovolemic shock has cut the fatality rate to less than 10 percent of even heavily envenomated patients; those who succumb are mostly children, whose body fluid volume is too small to accommodate the plasma leakage brought about by the toxins' perforation of their capillaries. Peripheral morbidity, including the loss of digits and even limbs, is still high, however, often aggravated by ill-advised first aid procedures (see Venom Poisoning).

***Abundance*** *C. atrox* is generally the most numerous venomous snake in the western two thirds of the state and, because of its bold temperament and frequently diurnal foraging pattern, one of the most likely to be noticed, especially around farm buildings that shelter rats and mice.

***Size*** Adults average 3 to 4 feet, yet because newborns are so numerous in early autumn, the majority of *atrox* encountered are less than 20 inches long. Huge western diamondbacks also occur rarely in the population, with several from the lower Rio Grande Valley measuring nearly 7½ feet. (Almost all such animals are radically stretched after death by being hung up for photographs, however, making their true size difficult to determine.) Since many diamondbacks have spent long lives—the record is nearly 26 years—in confinement without reaching remarkable size, extremely large specimens are true genetic giants rather than simply very old snakes. A new rattle segment is added each time a rattlesnake sheds its skin (which can happen up to 4 times a year), but because old rattles break off periodically like a too-long fingernail, the number of rattles is no indication of age.

***Habitat*** A sometime resident of nearly every terrestrial habitat within its range, *C. atrox* occurs in a variety of rural environments, especially where cover and small-mammal prey are available.

***Prey*** Diamondbacks feed mostly on mammals, from mice to, among the largest adults, cottontails and young jackrabbits; ground-living birds are also taken.

*RATTLESNAKES*

***Reproduction*** Live-bearing. Birth usually occurs in September, with litter size averaging 9 to 14; newborns are 9 to 13½ inches in length.

***Coloring/scale form*** Dorsal ground color varies markedly throughout the range; the light-edged, roughly diamond-shaped vertebral blotches tend to be so obscure on the posterior back that this reptile is most readily identified by its boldly black-and-white-banded "coon tail." A wide chocolate-gray band, its anterior and posterior edges lined with white, diagonally marks each cheek, obscuring the vertically slit-pupilled eye in a dusky mask. The pale forward border of this band intersects the upper lip midway along its length, while the white posterior cheek stripe runs from behind the eye straight to the corner of the mouth. The belly is unmarked yellowish white, with an undivided anal plate; the heavily keeled dorsal scales are arranged in 25 to 27 rows at midbody, and only 2 internasal scales intersect the rostral.

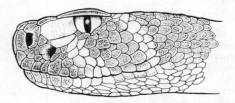

*Western diamondback rattler*

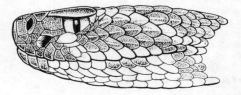

*Prairie and Mojave rattlers*

***Similar snakes*** The **prairie rattler (102)** is distinguished by its rounded brown vertebral blotches, which on its posterior trunk elongate into narrow crossbands separated by a tan ground color. Unlike the diamondback, the prairie has more than 2 internasal scales intersecting its rostral, while the white posterior border of its dark subocular band curves backward *above* the corner of its mouth. The **Mojave rattler (105),** found only northwest of Big Bend within 100 miles of the Mexican border, generally exhibits white tail bands much wider than its black caudal rings, as well as brownish vertebral diamonds that elongate on the rear third of its back (ahead of the tail) into crossbands similar to those of the prairie rattler; also like the prairie, it has a diagonal white postocular line that curves backward above the corner of its mouth. Most important, no more than 3 longitudinal rows of large, slightly roughened cephalic scales line the center of its anterior crown between the supraocular plates. See Mojave rattler (105) for illustration.

Both **northern blacktail (104)** and **timber (103) rattlers** have entirely dark, sooty tails, while **rock rattlesnakes (106–107)**, which have only 23 midbody rows of dorsal scales, also lack the diamondback's black-and-white-ringed tail, its partially white-edged anterior vertebral diamonds, and the white-bordered chocolate band below its eye. Unlike *Crotalus atrox*, the **massasaugas (108–109)** have heads capped with 9 large scale plates, numerous brown dorsal and lateral blotches, and brown-and-buff-banded tails.

***Behavior*** Western diamondbacks typically follow fairly structured seasonal activity patterns. Many winter in communal dens, sometimes for relatively brief periods, though they usually remain in the vicinity of their dens from the last week in October through March or April. During cold weather western diamondbacks engage in little hunting but are often active for a short, temperature-dependent period at midday, especially on the Rio Grande plain and coastal islands. With the advent of warm weather, *atrox* may move as far as 3 miles to their summer ranges, where by late May or June, their predatory forays have split into early morning and evening periods; during July and August high temperatures limit their foraging to a short period well after midnight, the coolest part of the day.

# Prairie Rattlesnake

*Crotalus viridis viridis*

**Venomous**    Findlay E. Russell's work with the toxins of *Crotalus viridis* (*Snake Venom Poisoning*, Philadelphia: Lippincott, 1980) indicates that the venom is slightly more lethal than that of the western diamondback rattler, mostly because of the prairie's much larger complement of neurotoxically active peptide components. (*Viridis* toxins have only about half the tissue-necrotizing effect and less than a third the blood-destroying potency of diamondback venom.) Yet the small stature of most prairie rattlers means that this species' average venom capacity ranges only from 35 to 110 milligrams (dry weight), compared to the diamondback's 175- to 600-milligram average.

**Abundance**    In much of the Panhandle *C. v. viridis* may be locally abundant, while on the western Stockton Plateau and in the Trans-Pecos, it is very uncommon.

**Size**    Although this slender pit viper reaches a maximum of just over 4½ feet, the majority are between 2 and 3 feet long.

**Habitat**    Prairie rattlers are widely distributed across the Great Plains from southeastern Alberta and Saskatchewan to northern Chihuahua, though their Texas range occupies only the southern tip of this long sweep of open country.

**Prey**    Prey is mostly small mammals and ground-dwelling birds; the young also take lizards.

**Reproduction**    Live-bearing. Gestating females observe an energy-conserving cycle of midday basking and nocturnal sheltering beneath the earth or beside sun-warmed stones, moving about very little and feeding rarely if at all during the final weeks before giving birth, in late August, September, and early October, to 8½- to 11-inch-long offspring.

**Coloring/scale form**    Thirty-five to 55 oval-shaped brown patches line the center of the back; frequently waisted over the spine anteriorly, these blotches elongate into narrow crossbands on the posterior third of the trunk. *C. v. viridis* is unique among native rattlers in having more than 2 internasal scales touching its rostral scale, while extending diagonally rearward along the cheeks, a pair of thin white seams—the higher of which curves backward above the corner of the mouth—border a dark subocular band. Arranged in 25 to 27 rows at midbody, *C. v. viridis*' dorsal scales are keeled, its unmarked belly is yellowish white, and its anal plate is undivided.

***Similar snakes*** The **western diamondback (101)** has wide black and white bands around its tail; diamond-shaped, dimly white-edged anterior vertebral blotches; 2 internasal scales intersecting its rostral; and a white upper cheek stripe that runs straight to the corner of its mouth. The **Mojave rattlesnake (105)** has wide white and narrower black tail bands and the same white-edged anterior vertebral diamonds as the diamondback. Two internasal scales touch its rostral, and a unique double or triple row of large, rough scales lines the center of its crown, where the prairie rattler has 4 or more rows of much smaller scales. The tail of the **northern blacktail rattlesnake (104)** is charcoal, the stripe through its eye is darker than that of the prairie rattler and devoid of white borders, a dark brown band along its spine encloses jagged-edged patches of paler scales, and 2 internasals touch its rostral. The **rock rattlesnakes (106–107)** lack the prairie's brown vertebral ovals as well as its white cheek stripes. These pale gray little reptiles are cross-barred with jagged black bands, possess only 23 rows of dorsal scales, and have but 2 internasal scales in contact with the rostral.

***Behavior*** Prairie rattlers are most active when temperatures range between 80 and 90 degrees Fahrenheit. In the northern portion of the range this makes for a fairly short annual activity period, but the prairie's defensive adaptations—among them its ability to threaten a potential adversary by noisily shaking the column of modified, hollow scales that tips its tail—combined with its predatory effectiveness in exploiting the rich bird and small-mammal life of the Great Plains, enable this warmth-loving reptile to range farther into Canada than any other serpent except the bullsnake, the hognoses, and the garter snakes.

# Timber Rattlesnake

*Crotalus horridus*

***Venomous***   The venom contains a larger percentage of neurotoxically active peptide components than the venom of the western diamondback, although its destructive effect on local tissue is only about two thirds as great; as a result, the overall potency of *C. horridus'* venom is probably no more than three quarters that of the diamondback's.

***Abundance***   Widely distributed across the eastern third of the state, but generally uncommon near human-populated areas.

***Size***   Most adult timber rattlers range from 30 to 48 inches in length; the record is just over 74 inches.

***Habitat***   The denser and more extensive the thicket, the better environment it generally affords *Crotalus horridus*, although in Texas, timber rattlers also occupy open, upland pine and deciduous woods and the second-growth pastures of unused farmland.

***Prey***   In the stomachs of 30 specimens taken in Louisiana were 10 rabbits, 8 mice, 6 rats, and 1 fox squirrel.

***Reproduction***   Live-bearing; an average brood numbers just over 10, born in late summer.

***Coloring/scale form***   The black tail, cinnamon vertebral stripe, and dark dorsolateral chevrons are definitive, while the dull whitish or yellowish belly may be faintly smudged along its edges with patches of darker pigment. Among the Texas population the keeled dorsal scales are arranged in 25 rows at midbody, although northern individuals sometimes have 23. Like that of all rattlesnakes, the anal plate is undivided.

***Similar snakes***   Herpetological opinion is divided over whether the southern form of the timber rattlesnake constitutes a subspecies **canebrake rattler,** *C. h. atricaudatus*, or is merely a variant color phase; those who define the canebrake as a separate subspecies do so on the basis of its color, its consistent 25 rows of dorsal scales, and the distinct boundary between its territory and that of the northern variety.

The only other rattlesnakes that share the timber rattler's Texas range are the **western massasauga (108)** and the **western pigmy rattler (110),** both smaller animals whose proportionately narrower crowns are striped with chocolate and, unlike the small-scaled forecrown of the timber, capped with 9 large scale plates. Their tails are banded with light and dark brown, while the pigmy has big dark dorsolateral spots, a tiny rattle, and 21 midbody rows of dorsal scales. The **western diamondback rattler (101)** is distinguished by its mottled gray-brown back dimly patterned with white-edged diamonds, its black-and-white-banded tail, and its white-bordered dark postocular stripe.

**Behavior**  Timber rattlers seem to be thinly dispersed in even the richest natural habitat. They are primarily nocturnal foragers, although before spring foliage has cut visibility in the woodland understory, an occasional individual can be seen basking in a patch of sunlight at the base of a tree or next to a log.

# Northern Blacktail Rattlesnake

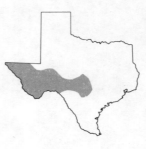

*Crotalus molossus molossus*

**Venomous**   The blacktail is generally less aggressive than the western diamondback, and since most *C. m. molossus* also inhabit relatively inaccessible terrain where they are difficult to approach, few bites are recorded for this species. Consequently, the specific pathology of the venom was little known until recently, when it was found to have a primary toxic effect of impairing blood coagulation, as well as a lethal potency some 79 percent that of the western diamondback.

**Abundance**   Found only occasionally in the canyons of the western Edwards Plateau, in mountainous parts of the Trans-Pecos *C. m. molossus* may be the most abundant rattler.

**Size**   The largest blacktail on record is the 52-inch-long male captured on Kerr County's South Fork Ranch; most adults are less than 32 inches in length, however.

**Habitat**   On the Edwards Plateau blacktails seek the heavily foliaged ledges of limestone canyons, while west of the Pecos River, *C. m. molossus* most often occurs in upland pine-oak forests, although rocky stream beds are also inhabited at lower elevations.

**Prey**   Primarily small mammals and, especially among juveniles, lizards.

**Reproduction**   Live-bearing. Two Brewster County females deposited litters of 7 and 8 young (all of which measured between 8 and 10¼ inches in length) in late July.

**Coloring/scale form**   The dark tail, forecrown, and spinal coloring, combined with patches of pale vertebral scales, is distinctive. The light vertebral scales are quite variable in color, with tan, olive (the green rattler of southwestern folklore is a blacktail), or grayish hues occurring among snakes living in the same county. A majority of blacktails have 27 midbody rows of keeled dorsal scales, although individuals vary between 25 and 29 rows. The belly has a yellow or even faintly greenish cast, clouded and mottled in places with gray, and the anal plate is undivided.

**Similar snakes**   No other western rattlesnake has a chocolate to black forecrown, a uniformly charcoal tail, or prominent patches of creamy scales enclosed by dark vertebral pigmentation.

**Behavior**   Blacktails in Texas seldom venture out of hiding until well after dark, often in cool weather: despite prevailing temperatures near 60 degrees, several Kerr County individuals were abroad as late as December 12; other fully active blacktails have been brought for identification to hill country high schools as early in the year as mid-February.

# Mojave
# Rattlesnake

*Crotalus scutulatus scutulatus*

**Venomous**   The Mojave rattler is probably the most dangerous serpent north of Mexico due to its combination of quick-striking defensive behavior and venom whose potency, among California populations at least, may approach that of the cobras. The venom's lethal dosage for a human adult is no more than 10 to 15 milligrams (dry weight), and a large specimen can be milked of up to 90 milligrams. Some evidence indicates that Arizona and New Mexico *scutulatus* have less virulent toxins, however, and it seems likely that in this respect Texas' Mojaves resemble their geographically closer kin.

**Abundance**   Only in the southwestern portion of Presidio, Brewster, and Jeff Davis counties is this species relatively abundant, being less common over the remainder of its limited range north of the Rio Grande.

**Size**   *C. s. scutulatus* is similar in conformation to the prairie rattler: relatively slender, with the majority of adults measuring less than 32 inches in length. The record is just over 54 inches.

**Habitat**   Along the Rio Grande to the west of Big Bend National Park, the Mojave's habitat consists mostly of nonrocky desert and creosote bush flats, but *C. s. scutulatus* is also present in rolling hills of mesquite and prickly pear near Marfa, as well as in the Davis Mountains.

**Prey**   Prey is primarily arid-terrain rodents such as ground squirrels, pocket gophers, and kangaroo, white-footed, and pocket mice.

**Reproduction**   Live-bearing. The only documented litter born in Texas is the brood conceived, after copulation on October 2, at the Fort Worth Zoo. The offspring were deposited 9½ months later on July 23 and measured 9.6 to 10.2 inches in length.

**Coloring/scale form**   The forward portion of the Mojave's back resembles that of the western diamondback; the posterior section is marked like a prairie rattler's. Narrow black and wide white bands encircle its tail, while the lower half of the basal rattle segment may have a yellowish hue much lighter than the rest of the rattle. The diagonal white line posteriorly bordering the brown subocular band passes rearward well above the corner of the Mojave's mouth, while between the big cephalic plates that cap its eyes a unique double (occasionally triple) row of enlarged, slightly roughened scales occupies the midsection of the crown. Arranged in 25 rows at midbody, the dorsal scales are keeled; the pale belly may be smudged along its edges; and as with all rattlers, the anal plate is undivided.

*RATTLESNAKES*

***Similar snakes*** The very similar **western diamondback (101)** is distinguishable by vertebral diamonds that fade posteriorly but do not elongate into distinct dark brown crossbands on the rear of the body and by its nearly equally wide black and white tail bands. Its upper postocular white line directly intersects the corner of its mouth, and 4 or more rows of very small scales cover its forecrown (see illustration).

The **prairie rattlesnake (102)** is unique in that more than 2 of its internasal scales touch its rostral, while its central forecrown, unlike the Mojave's, is evenly covered with 4 or more rows of little scales. *C. v. viridis'* dorsal foreparts are also patterned with rounded brown blotches unlike the Mojave's angular, white-edged diamonds. **Rock rattlers (106–107)** are smaller serpents with heavy dorsolateral speckling, irregular dark crossbands, and 23 midbody rows of dorsal scales; they also lack the Mojave's characteristic row of enlarged midcrown scales.

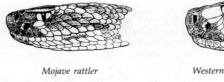

*Mojave rattler*          *Western diamondback rattler*

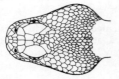
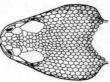

***Behavior*** When slightly threatened, adult Mojaves may lower their heads, raise their tails, and employ a slow and—in light of their extremely toxic venom—particularly menacing gesture, flicking their rattles from side to side as deliberately as a metronome.

# Mottled
# Rock
# Rattlesnake
## *Crotalus lepidus lepidus*

**Venomous**   Because deep penetration is not necessary to kill its diminutive prey, *Crotalus lepidus* (along with the pigmy rattler) has fangs smaller in relation to even its modest body size than those of any other pit viper in Texas. Evidence indicates, however, that its venom contains a high percentage of neurotoxically active components. The danger of being bitten is largely limited to reptile fanciers and zoo personnel, though, due to the rock rattler's comparatively inaccessible mountain and desert habitat, as well as to its ability to sense an intruder's heavy footsteps and its inclination to withdraw into crevices.

**Abundance**   In areas of suitable habitat mottled rock rattlers are not uncommon over much of the southwestern quarter of the state, and in some places they are quite numerous: to capture these colorful little vipers, enthusiasts used to cruise Trans-Pecos back roads, but both indigenous races are now protected in Texas.

**Size**   The smallest of West Texas' rattlesnakes, averaging under 2 feet in length; the record length is 32½ inches.

**Habitat**   This almost exclusively rock-dwelling animal is found primarily on canyon ledges and bluffs and in evergreen mountain woodland at altitudes above 2,500 feet, although open, stony desert is also inhabited.

**Prey**   Primarily lacertilian, including desert side-blotched and spiny lizards; snakes, mice, and occasional amphibians are also eaten.

**Reproduction**   Live-bearing. Its small litters mean that *C. lepidus* probably has the lowest reproductive rate of any indigenous viper. The young are born in mid- to late summer, 8 or 10 months after mating, with the earliest account of parturition coming from John Werler (Zoologica 36 [3]:37–48, 1951): "A 20.15-inch-long female [taken on] the Blackstone Ranch in Terrell County . . . gave birth to three young on July 21." The newborns averaged 8½ inches in length and differed from their pale, indistinctly banded parent in being "more vividly colored, with dark gray crossbands. Food taken includes young rusty lizards . . . and newborn mice."

**Coloring/scale form**   The highly variable pigmentation of Texas' celebrated pink and "little blue" rattlers serves as camouflage from both their color-visioned lizard quarry and their avian predators. Like many other reptiles, they have evolved coloring that in most cases closely matches the rocky terrain on which they live: dark primary blotches on a pink or buff ground hue characterize the population of the Davis Mountains, where dark-colored volcanic rock is prevalent, while those living along the Rio Grande, as well as on the Stockton and Edwards plateaus, occur on pale limestone and have ground colors of chalk to faintly bluish gray. The wedge-shaped crown is much wider

*RATTLESNAKES*

than the wiry neck and is covered with small scales; the conventional 2 internasal scales touch the rostral. The keeled dorsal scales are arranged in 23 rows at midbody, and the anal plate is undivided.

**Similar snakes**  *C. l. lepidus* differs from the **banded rock rattler (107)** in that among *lepidus lepidus* dark cross-dorsal bars occur mostly on the posterior body and there is considerable dark speckling of the pale ground color; against a predominantly unmottled ground color the banded race's black crossbands are distinct throughout its length. Adult *klauberi* also usually lack a dark postocular stripe, and the rear of the crown is likely to be marked with a pair of large brown spots absent in *lepidus lepidus*. The **desert massasauga (109),** a grassland serpent, is distinguished from the rock rattlers by its 9 large cephalic scale plates banded with a pair of brown stripes; both forms of *lepidus* also lack the massasauga's large brown dorsolateral spots. **Northern blacktail rattlesnakes (104)** have blackish tails and dark vertebral pigmentation patched with groups of pale scales; there are at least 25 midbody rows of dorsal scales. **Western diamondback rattlesnakes (101)** also have 25 to 27 dorsal scale rows; there are dimly white-edged anterior vertebral diamonds, no dark dorsolateral crossbands, and a white-bordered diagonal brown cheek stripe. **Mojave rattlesnakes (105)** are also distinguished by their large anterior vertebral diamonds edged with both light and dark scales, by their 25 midbody rows of dorsal scales, and by the double or triple row of enlarged, roughened scales that lines the middle of their forecrowns. Narrow white stripes also border the Mojave's dark cheek band, the upper stripe curving rearward above the corner of the mouth. The **prairie rattlesnake (102)** has oval brown blotches along the forward part of its spine; these elongate into transverse bands across the posterior body. More than 2 internasal scales contact the prairie's rostral, there are 25 to 27 rows of dorsal scales, and as with the diamondback and Mojave rattlers, a diagonal brown cheek band is outlined above and below with white seams.

**Behavior**  During summer, mottled rock rattlers—which are less nocturnal than many other crotalids—are most often abroad in early morning and around sunset, avoiding the midday heat by coiling against tree trunks or under rock overhangs or low bushes. Although inactive at these times, they are fully alert and poised to strike any lizard that darts through their patch of shade.

# Banded Rock Rattlesnake

*Crotalus lepidus klauberi*

**Venomous**   See mottled rock rattler (106).

**Abundance**   Uncommon as a pure race in Texas, this predominantly Mexican subspecies ranges northward into southern Arizona, New Mexico, and, at least as far as its genetic influence is concerned, the westernmost counties in Texas.

**Size**   The same as that of the mottled rock rattler (106).

**Habitat**   *C. l. klauberi*'s mountainous habitat is similar to that of the more eastern race.

**Prey**   Identical to that of the mottled rock rattler (106).

**Reproduction**   Live-bearing. Several captive broods of 2 to 5 have consisted of 7½-inch-long neonates (with yellowish tail tips) whose average birth weight has been just over a quarter-ounce.

**Coloring/scale form**   Often similar to the mottled rock rattler (106), although some specimens—such as the one pictured—are the most strikingly marked rattlesnakes found anywhere in the United States, with an unblemished silvery white back patterned solely by sawtooth-edged black crossbands.

**Similar snakes**   See mottled rock rattlesnake (106).

**Behavior**   Although wary, like other rock rattlers *C. l. klauberi* seems to have a characteristic curiosity, for it will withdraw into stony crevices less deeply than it might for its own protection in order to watch an intruder. During spring and fall as well as on overcast days, rock rattlers engage in extensive diurnal foraging, especially immediately after thunderstorms, when individuals emerge onto the still-moist rocks.

*RATTLESNAKES*

# Western Massasauga

*Sistrurus catenatus tergeminus*

**Venomous**  Despite the western massasauga's sporadic local abundance, few envenomations are recorded, since large human populations occur mainly in the southern segment of this little viper's Texas distribution, where it is now very uncommon. This retiring animal also tends to avoid human-inhabited areas, while its nocturnal habits—out of 60 recorded field observations, not a single instance of daytime activity was noted—further restrict *tergeminus'* opportunities for encounters with people. A major factor in the usually moderate toxic effect of massasauga envenomation is that these animals' venom capacity is so low: because only 15 to 45 milligrams (dry weight) can be obtained even by artificial milking, a bite lethal to a healthy human adult is highly unlikely.

**Abundance**  Now numerous only in scattered areas located mostly in the northern half of its range, a 200-mile-wide band of prairie running from the Gulf Coast to the northeastern Panhandle.

**Size**  Most adult *tergeminus* measure about 2 feet in length; the record is 34¾ inches.

**Habitat**  In Texas, western massasaugas are grassland animals that spend the daylight hours hidden either below ground or in dense clumps of prickly pear or bunchgrass.

**Prey**  Western massasaugas are opportunistic predators on a variety of small vertebrates: 18 stomachs contained 9 pocket and harvest mice, 3 whiptail and rusty lizards, 2 ground snakes, 1 lined snake, 2 leopard frogs, and a shrew.

**Reproduction**  Live-bearing. Breeding occurs both spring and fall, with the 7- to 9-inch young being born during July and August in litters of 5 to 13.

**Coloring/scale form**  The large, closely spaced brown dorsolateral spots are distinctive; the belly is mottled with gray-brown, though there is more light-colored pigment than dark. *Sistrurus* rattlesnakes are thought to be similar to the first rattlers to branch from their moccasinlike ancestors because they retain the 9 large forecrown scale plates of the copperheads and cottonmouths (see illustration). Arranged in 25 rows at midbody, the dorsal scales are keeled; the anal plate is undivided.

**Similar snakes**  The **desert massasauga (109)** is a slightly smaller, paler, arid-land race formally distinguished—though these distinctions do not hold true for many individuals—by its fewer (35 to 37) dorsal blotches on a creamy ground color, its uniformly white belly, and its 23 midbody rows of dorsolateral scales. Texas' other *Sistrurus* rattler is the **pigmy rattlesnake**

**(110)**, found in eastern woodland and along the Gulf Coast, where the generally upland-plains-living western massasauga rarely occurs. The pigmy is distinguished by a gray dorsolateral ground color punctuated by widely spaced blackish blotches, a dim russet-tan vertebral stripe, 21 rows of dorsal scales, and a diminutive rattle no longer than the distance between the eyes.

All other rattlesnakes within the western massasauga's range have their crowns covered with small scales. The **timber rattlesnake (103)** is a predominantly woodland reptile with a black tail; no broad stripes line its wide, triangular crown. Both the **western diamondback rattler (101)** and the **prairie rattler (102)** are larger, speckled and mottled above, with small-scaled crowns. The diamondback also has a black-and-white-ringed tail and the dimly white-bordered vertebral diamonds for which it is named, while the prairie, unlike the diamondback, has more than 2 internasal scales intersecting its rostral scale. The **prairie kingsnake (43)** and the **dusty (45)** and **plains (46) hognose snakes** are also similar to the western massasauga in dorsolateral coloring but lack the viper's rattle as well as the pronounced distinction between its narrow neck and broader crown, its heat-sensing facial pits, and its large, elliptically pupilled eyes.

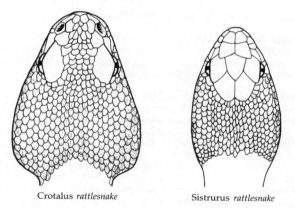

Crotalus *rattlesnake*          Sistrurus *rattlesnake*

**Behavior**   Since western massasaugas are apparently quite sensitive to elevated temperatures, with diminished activity above 93 degrees Fahrenheit, few are seen after hot weather begins. By July, even in areas where it was most abundant in late spring *S. c. tergeminus* seems to be almost nonexistent, although the first chill of autumn sometimes draws a few individuals back to the sun-warmed pavement just before they enter winter dormancy.

# Desert Massasauga

*Sistrurus catenatus edwardsii*

**Venomous**   While no record exists of human envenomation by this retiring little rattlesnake, the potency of its toxins is probably the same as for its subspecies, the western massasauga (108).

**Abundance**   Although it is distributed over a large range, the desert massasauga is not evenly dispersed and, except in particular local areas, is generally quite uncommon.

**Size**   Adult *S. c. edwardsii* average less than 18 inches in length, with the record specimen spanning only 20½ inches.

**Habitat**   This misleadingly named animal is most often an inhabitant of either shortgrass prairie (in the Panhandle and Trans-Pecos) or open thorn brush savannah (in South Texas).

**Prey**   *S. c. edwardsii* captured in the Tamaulipan community of the lower coastal plain choose laboratory mice as prey over reptiles or amphibians, but 2 adults captured in Presidio County would feed only on whiptail lizards.

**Reproduction**   Live-bearing. See western massasauga (108).

**Coloring/scale form**   Essentially a pale replica of the western race with fewer (35 to 37), more widely spaced and less contrasting brown vertebral blotches, a creamy ground color, and a uniformly white belly. There are 23 rows of keeled dorsal scales and the anal plate is undivided.

**Similar snakes**   The desert massasauga is the only rattler within its range whose head is capped with the 9 large scale plates typical of its genus. The **western diamondback (101)** has a mottled grayish back patterned with dimly white-edged vertebral diamonds, 25 to 27 dorsal scale rows at midbody, and a distinctly black-and-white-ringed tail; the **prairie rattler (102)** also has 25 to 27 rows of dorsal scales at midbody and numerous small cephalic scales between the large supraocular scales that flank its broad, triangular crown. More than 2 internasal scales intersect its rostral. **Mottled (106)** and **banded (107) rock rattlers** have dark-mottled pale gray or pinkish-brown backs with jagged black posterior crossbands, as well as tails whose wide pale interspaces separate blackish rings. The **northern blacktail rattlesnake (104)** has a dark forecrown, blackish vertebral pigmentation that encloses patches of paler scales, and a charcoal-colored tail. Also similar in appearance to the desert massasauga are the **western hognoses (45–47)** and the **Great Plains rat snake (41)**—among small massasaugas the rattle is evident only upon close examination.

**Behavior**   This nocturnal reptile is ordinarily seen only in the evening, when individuals appear coiled on the edges of the road.

# Western Pigmy Rattlesnake

*Sistrurus miliarius streckeri*

**Venomous**   Partly because *S. miliarius'* diminutive jaws and fangs—the latter no more than ⁵⁄₃₂ inch across the curve—limit it to superficial penetration of the human body, bites by pigmy rattlers almost never result in the extensive tissue death characteristic of envenomation by larger crotalids. Further, even when their venom glands are artificially milked to depletion, the biggest *S. miliarius* yield no more than 35 milligrams (dry weight) of venom—nearly 3 times as much as the snake could expel on its own but still less than half the probable lethal dose for an adult human being.

**Abundance**   Uncommon. Poorly dispersed throughout its broad East Texas range, the western pigmy rattler is nevertheless sometimes so abundant locally that in biologically generous environments it can be one of the most numerous venomous serpents. Yet even where it is common, *S. m. streckeri* is rarely seen, since it spends the day hidden beneath ground cover.

**Size**   Adult *S. m. streckeri* are short and plump, averaging no more than 14 to 20 inches in length; the record is 25⅛ inches.

**Habitat**   Two primary macrohabitats are occupied: the eastern loblolly pine and hardwood community, particularly where the understory vegetation is wire grass and palmetto, and the upper Texas coastal plain where there is both heavy vegetation and abundant surface water. In addition, the riparian corridor of sycamore, pecan, black willow, and mustang grape that traces the Trinity and Red river systems allows these fundamentally eastern forest animals to range westward throughout an extensive upland area.

**Prey**   Because much of the warm-blooded prey taken by larger vipers is too big for pigmy rattlers, small reptiles, amphibians, and insects—the typical food of most juvenile crotalids—constitute much of the diet of even adult *S. miliarius*. Thirteen dusky pigmy rattlesnakes from Georgia contained 4 large centipedes, 3 ground skinks, 1 six-lined racerunner lizard, 1 ringneck snake, and 2 deer mice.

**Reproduction**   Live-bearing. A captive pair maintained at the Fort Worth Zoo bred repeatedly throughout September, with the female giving birth some 8½ months later to a litter of three ¹⁄₁₀-ounce, 5⅓-inch-long young with pale yellow tail tips.

*RATTLESNAKES*

*Coloring/scale form*   The gray back is spotted with black, there is a russet-tan vertebral stripe, and the lower sides are marked by a row of dark spots that may overlap onto the otherwise whitish or faintly stippled belly. *Miliarius'* tiny rattle—no longer than the distance between its eyes—is so nearly inaudible that anyone able to hear it in the field is in danger of being bitten on the ear, giving rise to the myth of the rattleless ground rattler. The strongly keeled dorsal scales are arranged in 21 rows at midbody and the anal plate is undivided, while the crown is covered with 9 large scale plates, like that of the massasaugas.

*Similar snakes*   The **western massasauga (108)** has larger, much more closely spaced brown dorsolateral blotches; it lacks a distinct vertebral stripe and is almost never found in the pigmy rattler's woodland or coastal wetland habitat. It has 25 rows of dorsal scales at midbody, and its rattle is larger and its dark horizontal cheek band wider than the pigmy's. Except as juveniles, **timber (103)** and **diamondback (101) rattlesnakes** are larger serpents with (in Texas) at least 25 midbody rows of dorsal scales, as well as very small scales covering the center of their broad crowns. The timber rattler is also jaggedly crossbarred with dark brown chevrons and has a uniformly blackish tail, while the diamondback's tail is ringed with black and white.

*Behavior*   Although extremely retiring, pigmy rattlesnakes often respond pugnaciously if disturbed, puffing the body in threat and snapping sharply sideways without coiling. The strike never spans more than a few inches, however, since pigmies do not assume the raised-forebody defensive posture of *Crotalus* rattlers.

# GLOSSARY

**adhesive-shelled eggs**   Eggs with a sticky surface that causes them to adhere in a cluster when laid; the shells soon dry out, but the eggs remain stuck together.

**aestivation**   The dry- or hot-weather-induced dormancy of many reptiles and amphibians.

**amphiuma**   A large, eellike aquatic salamander with small legs and no external gills.

**anal plate**   The scale covering the vent, or anus.

**anaphylaxis**   An antigen-antibody reaction caused by hypersensitivity to a foreign protein such as antivenin; capable in extreme cases of producing severe shock, respiratory impairment, coma, and death.

**anchor coil**   The lowermost loop of the trunk, which serves the pit viper as a foundation from which to launch its strike.

**annelid**   Any segmented worm or leech; most commonly the earthworm.

**anterior**   Toward the head.

**antibody**   A globulin produced in reaction to the introduction of a foreign protein.

**antiserum**   The fluid portion of the blood of an animal previously infused with a reactive foreign protein.

**antivenin**   Crystallized serum produced from the antibodies of animals infused with venom; able to partly neutralize venom's metabolism of its victim's tissue by blocking the toxic enzymes' access to their target cells.

*Antivenin Index*   A compendium of antivenins available in the United States (including those for exotic serpents) published by the Oklahoma Poison Information Center and the Oklahoma State Department of Health in Oklahoma City. Antivenin for native North American pit viper and coral snake venoms is produced by Wyeth Laboratories in Philadelphia.

**anuran**   A frog or toad.

**arachnid**   An eight-legged invertebrate: spiders, scorpions, mites, and ticks.

**arthropod**   Any segmented invertebrate with jointed legs: insects, arachnids, and crustaceans.

**azygous scale**   A single (that is, not one of a bilateral pair) scale.

**belly line**   The horizontal line of intersection between the belly and the lower sides.

**brumation**   The winter dormancy of reptiles and amphibians.

**caudal**   Pertaining to the tail.

**cephalic**   Pertaining to the head or crown.

**chin shields**   The central scales on the underside of the lower jaw.

**chthonic**   Below or within the earth.

**cloaca**   The intestinal cavity into which the genital and urinary tracts open in birds, reptiles, and amphibians.

**colubrid**   A member of the largest worldwide family of snakes (Colubridae); most North American species are harmless.

**compartment syndrome**   The pressure of extreme edema, which after severe en-venomation may rarely cut off blood flow to a limb, causing the death of its tissue. Some authorities believe this to be a major cause of local necrosis that often warrants surgical alleviation by fasciotomy; most maintain that necrosis is due almost exclusively to the enzymatic, digestive action of the venom itself.

**corticosteroid**   A steroid, often used to treat venom poisoning, that originates in the adrenal cortex and whose effects include the enhancement of protein replacement, the reduction of inflammation, and the suppression of the body's immune responses.

**crepuscular**   Active mainly at dusk or dawn.

**crossband**   A band running across the back from the belly line on one side to the belly line on the opposite side.

**crotalid**   A pit viper: in North America, rattlesnakes, the cottonmouth, and the copperhead.

**cryotherapy**   The treatment of an injury with cold. Dangerous when a snakebitten extremity is radically chilled for several hours, since it can result in tissue death, although a cold pack on the wound may slightly reduce pain; and another on the forehead may help to offset the nausea that often accompanies poisoning by pit vipers.

**debridement**   The surgical removal of (venom-saturated) tissue.

**dichromatism**   The presence of 2 color phases within a species or subspecies.

**diel**   Daily or daytime.

**disjunct**   Geographically separate.

**distally**   Toward the sides of the body.

**diurnal**   Active mainly during the day.

**dorsal**   Pertaining to the back.

**dorsolateral**   Pertaining to the back and sides.

**dorsum**   The back and upper sides.

**Duvernoy's gland**   A gland that produces some of the venom of rear-fanged colubrid snakes; named for the French anatomist D. M. Duvernoy, who first described it.

**ecdysis**   The shedding of a reptile's outer skin; see exuviation.

**ecotone**   The transition zone between differing biological communities, such as the border between forest and meadow.

**ectotherm** An animal whose temperature is almost entirely determined by its environment.

**edema** The swelling of tissue due to the release of fluids, primarily from the vascular and lymph systems into the interstitial tissue spaces.

**egg-bearing** See oviparous.

**elapid** A rigidly front-fanged serpent of the family Elapidae, such as the coral snake, characterized by its large proportion of neurotoxically active venom fractions.

**endotherm** An internally heat-regulating animal.

**envenomation** The infusion of venom.

**enzyme** An organic agent capable of producing, by catalytic action, the metabolic breakdown of tissue into its component proteins.

**exuviation** A shed; the sloughing of the entire outer covering, or *stratum corneum*, of a snake's body, in a process that can occupy from 10 minutes to 6 hours. This first occurs within a few days of birth, then takes place every 4 to 14 weeks (less often as the snake grows older) throughout the animal's foraging period. Rattlesnakes add a new rattle segment with each exuviation; the terminal segments are periodically broken off.

**fasciotomy** A surgical incision into the fascial band enclosing a muscular compartment in an attempt to prevent tissue destruction from excessive hydraulic pressure. (This pressure is caused mostly by the fluid released by the venom's perforation of the capillary walls and pumped into the tissues by the heart.) It is of highly questionable value except as an emergency measure to save a limb in immediate danger of general necrosis due to vascular constriction.

**form** Subspecies or race.

**fossorial** Adapted to burrowing; subterranean.

**frontal scale** The large scale(s) located on the crown between the eyes.

**genotype** The genetic makeup of an individual.

**gravid** Pregnant.

**hemotoxic** Poisonous to or destructive of the blood, blood cells, or vascular system.

**hemipene** The Y-shaped penis of serpents and lizards.

**hypovolemic shock** Shock due to a loss of fluid from the circulatory system. In snakebite, this occurs when the arteriole and venule walls are perforated by venom enzymes.

**intergradation** The gradual genetic alteration of one subspecies into another across a geographical continuum.

**intergrade** An intermediate form exhibiting a combination of the characteristics of 2 or more subspecies.

**internasal scales** The scales just posterior to the rostral scale on top of the snout, anterior to the prefrontals.

**Jacobson's organs** A double-sided sensory organ located in the roof of the mouth of serpents and some lizards into which the tips of their forked tongues are pressed in order to both smell and taste the scent particles the tongue has picked up from air and ground.

**keel** The small ridge creasing the longitudinal centerline of a scale.

**labial scales** The large scales lining the margins of the upper and lower jaws.

**lacertilian** Pertaining to lizards.

**lateral** Pertaining to the sides.

**ligature** The binding of a limb with a narrow, radically circulation-impairing band such as a tourniquet.

**live-bearing** See ovoviviparous.

**loreal scale**   The scale between the preocular and nasal scales.

**lysis**   The breakdown or digestive metabolism of cells or tissue by a peptide or enzyme.

**maxillary bones**   The paired bones at the front of the upper jaw that in anterior-fanged venomous snakes carry the fangs. In the pit vipers, they are also able to rotate outward individually, swinging the fang tips forward.

**mesic**   Well watered.

**midventral**   Pertaining to the center of the belly.

**nasal scales**   The scales through which the nostrils open.

**necrosis**   The death of bone or soft tissue.

**neurotoxic**   Destructive primarily by impairing neuromuscular function; ophidian neurotoxins block the acetycholine receptor sites of the upper spinal ganglia.

**nuchal**   Pertaining to the neck.

**ocular scale**   The scale covering the eye.

**ophidian**   Pertaining to snakes.

**ophiophagous**   Feeding on snakes.

**oviparous**   Egg-bearing (producing eggs that hatch outside the body).

**ovoviviparous**   Live-bearing (retaining the membrane-encased embryos within the body until the deposition of fully developed young).

**parietal scales**   The pair of large scales located at the rear of the crown.

**parotid gland**   The organ that secretes saliva in mammals and most of the venom in both pit vipers and elapids such as the coral snakes.

**phenotype**   The physical characteristics of an organism.

**plates**   The large scales covering the crown and belly.

**polyvalent antivenin**   An antivenin produced from a combination of antibodies and therefore useful against the venom of an entire genus of snakes. For example, Wyeth's polyvalent antivenin is a single crystallized serum developed to treat the bites of all North American pit vipers: rattlesnakes, copperheads, and cottonmouths.

**posterior**   Toward the tail.

**postocular scales**   The scales bordering the posterior edge of the eye.

**prebutton**   The small, hornlike scale at the tip of a newborn rattler's tail.

**prefrontal scales**   The cephalic scales just anterior to the frontal plate.

**preocular scales**   The scales bordering the anterior edge of the eye.

**proteinase**   Any proteolytic, or tissue-dissolving, enzyme.

**proteolysis**   The destruction of tissue due to the inability of venom-weakened cell walls to withstand their internal fluid pressures.

**range**   The usual geographic distribution of an organism.

**relict population**   A contemporary remnant group of a species formerly found over a much broader range.

**rostral scale**   The scale covering the tip of the snout, frequently enlarged among burrowing species.

**saxicolous**   Rock-living.

**scute**   A large scale, or plate.

**serosanguinous**   Swollen with blood.

**sexual dimorphism**   A difference in coloring, pattern, size, or configuration according to gender.

**siren**   A large aquatic North American salamander shaped like an eel but possessing forelegs and external gills.

**Squamata**   The order comprising snakes and lizards.

**subocular scales**   The small scales separating the lower edge of the eye from the upper labials.

**supraocular scales**   The enlarged scales on the sides of the crown above the eyes.

**sympatric**   Having overlapping or corresponding ranges.

**temporal scales**   The scales along the side of the head behind the postocular scale(s) and between the parietals and the upper labials.

**terminal segment**   In rattlesnakes, the last rattle segment in the string. Because rattles break off periodically, there are rarely more than 8 or 10 segments in a series no matter how old the snake. See exuviation.

**thermoregulation**   An ectothermic animal's control of its body temperature by moving toward or away from warmer or cooler areas.

**venom fractions**   The approximately 3 dozen discrete toxic proteins—principally peptides and enzymes—that make up reptile venoms. Most of these fractions can be isolated from the venom mix by electrophoresis and dialysis.

**vent**   The posterior opening of the cloaca; the anus.

**venter**   The belly.

**ventral**   Pertaining to the belly.

**ventral scales**   The big, transversely elongate scale plates or scutes that line the underbody of most snakes.

**ventrolateral**   On the outer edge of the belly and the lower sides.

**vertebral**   Along the spine.

**vomeronasal organs**   Jacobson's organs.

**xeric**   Arid.

# INDEX

*NOTES*